AKASHIC RECORDS: GEMSTONE GUARDIANS

HEALING MESSAGES TO OVERCOME FEAR,
NAVIGATE CHANGE, AND CHOOSE THE
EVOLUTION OF YOUR PERSONAL POWER

CHERYL MARLENE

AKASHIC RECORDS:
Gemstone Guardians

Healing Messages to Overcome Fear,
Navigate Change, and Choose the
Evolution of Your Personal Power

CHERYL MARLENE

Akashic Records: Gemstone Guardians
Healing Messages to Overcome Fear, Navigate Change, and Choose the
Evolution of Your Personal Power

Published by
Soul Bright Press

Ebook ISBN:
978-1-945868-38-2
Paperback ISBN:
978-1-945868-39-9
Hardcover ISBN:
978-1-945868-40-5

CONTENTS

AKASHIC RECORD INSIGHTS

Looking to learn more?

AkashicRecordsInsights.com

**Where Inquiry Meets Illumination -- Personal
Transformation through the Ancient Wisdom of the
Akashic Records**

**Akashic Records Insights offers an extensive collection
of articles, new practices, workshops, and workbooks:**

AkashicRecordInsights.com

INTRODUCTION

The world is changing right before our hearts and minds. With such an intentional rhythm and a fast pace, global shift is obvious.

Held within is another shift: the present moment awareness of change. For change is with us always. However, change shouldn't be ignored or denied.

We can't pretend otherwise. We can't hide in the flow hoping life will always be what we can predict and control.

In this global shift, the awareness of time has compacted.

Gone are the days of the five-year plan based on certainty. Gone are specific to-do lists which guarantee outcome. Gone are the illusions of mastery by the rote following of your guru's advice.

The plan, the list, and the advice were all illusions — all hiding the truth of you behind a false promise of certainty.

For what has always been certain is your personal power — your capacity to live your life based on your truth. To make choices for yourself. To find safety within the turmoil.

When the sands of external certainty shift and seem to pull the rug of life out from under you, you have a choice.

You can choose to blame and get stuck in the junkyard of the past.

You can choose fear and chain yourself to a future loop which will never happen except in your frozen, panicked mind.

OR . . . .

You can choose the best of you: your truth born of your capacity, your power within, your self-determination to live the expression of your best self, here, now.

Some will not find a way past the fear of creating life through personal choice.

Some cannot break the habit of blame and accept personal responsibility.

The now-broken, externalized promise of certainty can be too shiny to ignore and discard.

Personal choice takes bravery and vulnerability.

There are no guarantees on this road of personal power within.

There are no absolutes based on a set of predefined rules or laws or commandments.

There is you and your willingness to venture with anticipation into the unknown.

Why do the impossible?

Simple.

You are capable of miracles.

You!

Not because you follow the promise of external authority.

Instead, because, one day, in one moment, you chose you for you.

A choice not based on false guarantees.

Rather a choice based on a willingness to trust yourself.

Why this choice?

Because within the change in your life your focus has shifted inward.

A shift toward your belief in yourself.

A shift to trust you.

A shift to focus on living from your power within.

The shifting sands are still there and will not fade.

The unknown and the unexpected will still butt in and shake things up.

Yet as inner power blossoms, personal resilience builds, self-trust strengthens, and personal choice becomes your go-to.

Come what may, you now have the resources to respond from the best of you in the face of unprecedented change.

Speaking from the truth in their hearts, the Gemstone Guardians offer support in these turbulent moments of massive global shift.

Know the motion without reflects the motion within. However, for you, the most important battle is not the external conflict.

Your primary personal challenge is the one of personal power within.

Within you is your choice, your self-determination, your autonomy to live life within the expression of your best self. Within is the creative engine of your personal power ready to fuel you to undertake the challenges born both within self and within this amazing universe.

The energy kingdom of Gemstones is powered by divine, universal awareness focused in our physical world through the physical presence of a multitude of gemstones. Borne of both physical and spiritual processes, gemstones are uniquely positioned to both understand our personal challenges and envision paths of possibility which answer our dreams.

In this book, thirty Gemstones have stepped forward within the Akashic Records to offer their soul story. Their assistance guides you to connect with your soul and integrate personal awareness, physical experience, and spiritual understanding across all levels, body, mind, heart, and soul.

From each is a heart-felt message to help you navigate global shift, overcome fear, and make powerful, heart-guided life choices.

For each speaks not to instruct you in exact steps.

Instead, each message intends to support the emergence and discovery within of your power, your self-belief, and your personal truth.

Messages to empower your best self with trust, confidence, and choice.

Messages of love to you, for you.

Learn. Laugh. Love. Be. Become. Always!

In Joy!

Cheryl

WHAT IS A GEMSTONE GUARDIAN?

Whenever I begin in the Akashic Records, I always define terms to make sure I am getting to the deeper energetic layers of the topic before me. More importantly, I want to ensure I am not blinded by my assumptions. I want to begin with clarity. I want to open the door wide for new perspectives and deepest understanding.

As an Akashic Mystic, I connect with the Akashic Records on a daily basis for myself and for others. I have done this for over 25 years and have specialized in many aspects including a unique and innovate understanding of the energetic nature of the Akashic Records.

Additionally, I have pushed into multiple avenues of Akashic Records connection – especially the energy I refer to as "of the Other." In this context, Other means all other flows of energy which are not you. This includes other people plus an infinite flow of non-human energy.

Historically, many came to believe that access to the Akashic Records were limited to past life information. My path of experience with the Akashic Records has proven this as an outdated fallacy. In fact, instead of a book in a heavenly library, the Akashic Records are a personal spiritual process which includes access to a divine source of knowing, healing, and spiritual practice.

My investigation of Other within the Akashic Records has taken me into amazing interactions with non-human energy, with both terrestrial and non-terrestrial energy, beyond the local of this dimension into the non-locality of all that exists beyond Physical Reality. One of my primary explorations has been with Gemstones.

For example, within the Akashic Records, there is a difference between opening the Akashic Records of this piece of amethyst held in my hand and the Akashic Records of all Amethyst. The specific focus is much like opening for one person versus the general focus of humanity.

Despite the differences, the first issue to be tackled within the Akashic Records of Gemstones is permission. Within my Agreements with the Akashic Records is the stipulation that I must be asked before opening for a human being. Within non-human energy if there is no legal authority, I must seek permission through my Akashic Records.

Within this process of seeking permission, my Akashic Records introduced me to the Gemstone Guardians and the Council of the Gemstone Guardians. Through these Akashic Records-based sources I have learned all knowing shared within this book. The creation and writing of this book has been a co-creative process of sharing the knowing of the Gemstone Guardians and my experience, learning, and truth as a human being and as an Akashic Mystic.

Gemstone Defined

For the purposes of this book and within the perspective of the Akashic Records, this is the definition of an Earth-based Gemstone:

> In response to divine soul intention, any physically solid material formed within the spiritual and physical creation process of Earth willing to conductively share the energy of its soul with humanity.

This is a broad definition which will allow the presence of stones or materials not generally included as a gemstone. But that is part of the point of this work with the Gemstone Guardians. We are both present to widen our minds and open our hearts to possibility – especially possibility coming from new or unexpected directions.

Gemstone Guardian Defined

As I have already noted, gemstones have both an individual perspective and a group soul perspective. The origin energy of the group is connected guardian energy.

Thus, a Gemstone Guardian holds the sacred soul energy of a gemstone. Said another way: a Gemstone Guardian is the original soul energy perspective of a gemstone which forms the integration of spiritual and physical experience of the gemstone. A Gemstone Guardian understands and supports the creative intent and the blocks and opportunities held within the intent of the gemstone.

Held within guardian energy, each gemstone emerges through an energy cascade initiated by intention. Each gemstone has its own personal creation story, its own soul journey – just like each human being.

Council of Gemstone Guardians Defined

In addition, there is a Council of Gemstone Guardians which is composed of many Gemstone Guardians as well as representatives from other councils such as Elements, Angelic, Akashic Archive, Earth Humanity, as well as Divine Mother and Ancient Mother. The Council also has Masters from multiple dimensions and parallels.

Within this book is the message of the Council of the Gemstone Guardians as well as the soul messages from thirty Gemstone Guardians. The intention of these messages is to aid and provide possibilities to transform within global shift, overcome fear, and experience the evolving nature of personal power within.

Each message comes from questions asked to all Guardians and each message concludes with questions you may ask yourself in meditative reflection or within your Akashic Records.

Though each message is relevant to our times, each is meant to help you connect with the timelessness of you integrated, body, mind, heart, and soul.

FROM THE COUNCIL OF THE GEMSTONE GUARDIANS

Surrounding you with love and light, please know that humanity on Earth is amid a very important change with two important aspects.

First, this shift is moving humanity towards life engaged within physical-spiritual integration. No longer stuck in the narrow dimensions of body and mind, humanity is entering into life lived within full integration on all levels, body, mind, heart, and soul.

Second is a shift in the way humanity perceives truth. What has been common is to see truth as that which is carved in stone, unchangeable, externalized, accessible to only a chosen few.

We see the experience of truth changing, becoming more an inner personal experience because each person is discovering and recognizing personal truth within.

Religious or social authority is not necessary as an intermediary to see and understand truth. Instead, truth is expressed within a person through their own experience and awareness, through their own open heart and clear mind.

This is a time of incredible contrasts – both reversal and moving forward.

The polarity of right and wrong is deepening and shifting. The power dynamics of Power-Over is loosening its hold on humanity. Gaining ascendancy are the dynamics of Power-With and Power-Within.

Our mandate as the Council of the Gemstone Guardians is to provide support to humanity during this change, to help facilitate understanding, to be real and honest.

> Each gemstone has their perspective.
> Each gemstone has their story.
> Each gemstone has their message for humanity.
> Together we describe a pathway to understand what
> is shifting and how this change is emerging.

Within Earth's current written history, this is the first period of human existence with this huge, swift transition.

Even just one hundred years from now, the way humanity lives on the planet will be very, different – beyond imagination – than life right now.

However, the energy of gemstones is not stagnant or set.

Our energy is infinitely more fluid than usually perceived. There is much more than this one is for healing and this one for clear sight. For like you, we are here to evolve our own expression and experience, and to share this evolution with you.

As part of the energetic matrix called Earth, our presence creates a particular type of energy awareness. We are also deeply connected and aligned with the work of Ancient Mother (the primordial progenitor of all Earth), and of Mother Earth and Planet Earth (reference to both the spiritual and physical aspects of the planet).

All Gemstones work together in harmony to support the deepest expressions both physically and spiritually, body, mind, heart, and soul of all humanity and of all energetic flows with which we share interconnection.

Because of this perspective, we are very aware of the motion of fear on the planet, though we do not engage in this fear.

This lack of engagement with fear is why human beings will find our energy so compelling and supportive. We do not contain fear. We are not driven by fear. Instead, we can observe fear and its push and drive. We can open pathways for fear's release.

We are in a constant state of harmony and balance. We thrive and have no worries about our survival.

As witnesses to the human experience, we understand what drives humanity to respond in fear and worry and concern.

We hope that our words will provide support and understanding.

As a Council and as Gemstones speaking in one voice, this is our broadest message to humanity:

> You do not need to live in fear.
> You do not need to believe that being driven by fear
> is the only path to survival.
> Fear does not need to drive choice.

When fear and the threat of survival is what drives your choices and what drives your ability to live your life, you are pushed outside of yourself. You are pushed to protect and to control, to ward off attack and the demand to give up the truth of you.

Fear manipulates, coerces, and tries to replace your own inner sense of personal power and truth with outside authority. What is within you is diminished in favor of external authority.

The energy of our souls shared through connection communicates about how the flow of our energy fields assist you to overcome fear and begin to live life within physical-spiritual integration. All gemstones have the capacity to help humanity develop a new expression of being human. We support unlimited experience of life on Earth and with the infinitely and eternally connected flow of All That Is.

This is experience of personal power. An experience where the interior sense of power within begins a path away from fear and toward personal trust and truth. Connection with gemstone energy helps the process of inner power become more fluid and feel more reliable even in tough moments.

Outside turmoil becomes less of a direct threat. The most effective personal response to global shift and change is to look inward and feel your power within. Beyond the control of fear, you can find peace and support through your own personal work.

The message from each of the Gemstone Guardians contained in this book focus on the release of fear and the encouragement and support for the inner process of deep, spiritual work.

We are with you and stand witness to your incredible journey of personal power within.

1

QUARTZ
CLEAR LIGHT

A common rock-forming mineral consisting of silica, SiO2, occurring as colorless hexagonal prisms. The word quartz is a borrowing from German quarz *– perhaps a pet form of* twerc, *dwarf.*

In my journey within the Akashic Records, I began with Quartz. In the first months of my study, I held a piece of quartz in my hand to help with clarity within me and within my connection with the Akashic Records. In my exploration, the Gemstone Guardians of Quartz were the first to introduce themselves to me.

I feel an affinity with this gemstone which still provides a focus of clarity. In the hexagonal formation, I feel a familiar energy which has connected me over time with other Gemstones. I find guidance to see things as they are instead of insisting on what I want it to be. The clarity provides support and reassurance. Quartz brings me to a point of calm even in the midst of storm.

Quartz was the first gemstone expression in the very first incarnation of Earth.

Quartz is about the clarity of heat, resilience through pressure, and the ability to withstand fear which pushes to annihilate or obliterate.

Quartz holds the foundation for all gemstones to express their individual natures and their individualized mandates for interaction with humanity.

However, Quartz in its first motion into physical form did not have the clarity or awareness we now possess. Through the first experience on Earth, Quartz attained animation and was able to demonstrate the possibilities of clarity and clairsentience available within the energy of all gemstones.

Quartz founded the Gemstone Guardian Council. Quartz held space for and educated other gemstones to accept their individual possibilities and mandates. This awareness cannot be forced upon any physical expression and must be arrived at with clear intention.

Through this experience with other Gemstone, Quartz developed the capacity to help people be clearly aware of intention. The primary motion of Quartz on Earth is to find, create, and hold foundation for clear awareness and clear knowing within any physical expression. Though Quartz intention is not limited to humanity.

As Earth has evolved, Quartz has evolved and expanded the foundation to support higher and deeper levels of intention and awareness.

As humanity moves into this period of physical-spiritual integration, Quartz is the primary gemstone to support clear intention within this process. This is a clarity that's not only physical but also spiritual. Quartz supports each human being to integrate clearly and functionally on all levels body, mind, heart, and soul.

The point of spiritual balance with Quartz is held within a sense of clarity and intention.

Our message for humanity is:

Light brings clarity and helps eliminate fear.

When there is turmoil within, Quartz can help clear the turmoil plus reduce the worry and concern of the unknown.

Quartz energy is focused on awareness in the moment and the light which can be focused on the next step, reducing anxiety over not reaching a desired destination.

We are here to support clarity and intention for your journey and the possibilities of this moment for your next step. Destination provides direction for intention. However, with present moment awareness, intention can shift as needed instead of being held hostage by the last moment's view of destination.

We are here with love and light – however you choose to express yourself, we can help clear fear.

Your way forward is to move beyond the limitations of fear. Think of fear as the opposite of light or the opposite of clarity. Fear is also the opposite of essential expression of authenticity.

Quartz is here to hold a light for you to find your authenticity. Quartz energy empowers you to find that place within you which is no longer oppressed by fear.

We also are here to help clear all that is not yet known or understood.

Even though Quartz's mandate is clarity, assistance from Quartz begins with what is not known, with what is troubling, with what is in doubt.

To get to clarity in the moment, personal focus begins with personal awareness – your attention toward the issue at hand.

Quartz brings awareness of What Is for you in the moment, however troubling or enlightening the awareness may be.

Quartz helps you to not get ahead of the moment, moving from mindless reaction to thoughtful response, shifting focus to the next step rather than producing a giant leap to an assumed destination.

Quartz also assists in anchoring personal power. The emergence of your personal power comes through your ability to trust yourself. To establish trust, you need a sense of clarity, a belief you can see whatever tries to obscure your awareness.

Our energy, based on clarity and light, opens doors and erases blocks. Within the Akashic Records or by physically holding a piece of Quartz, you can connect to our energy of clarity, directing it to you and the troublesome, fearful issue at hand.

Interaction with Quartz is turning on the light or shining light in the darker corners of personal awareness. Truth exists within you as an intrinsic element of your humanity. The energy flow of Quartz helps you enlighten the darkness so you may embrace truth without fear.

Remember, fear has two primary sources: within and without. Without means that another person or event is trying to convince you that fear is the most reasonable choice within the circumstances. There will be challenge, intimidation, and coercion.

However, in most cases, this fear is false interpretation or outright lies and certainly not in your highest interest. This is fear as a tool of manipulation to get you to choose in a way you wouldn't if you understood you were being intimidated by falseness. Most often, this fear is raised to scare you about a group of people or a particular outcome. You will know this fear without because it comes from outside of you and tries to drag you into a future filled with the falseness of its manipulation.

Fear within is a natural human reaction to an unknown future. This is where the power of the present moment is so important. For it is in the present, and with clarity, you can see the truth of the fear for yourself.

Remember, an empowered life is not about eliminating fear. The empowered life looks fear in the face and sidesteps its manipulative attempts.

Rather, within fearful moments, personal power is found within choice. Choice is always available. Exercising choice is the first step in confronting fear. Choice allows you to respond within clarity instead of within the mindless, heartless push of fear, especially fear without.

Remember:

Light brings clarity and helps eliminate fear.

Personal Exploration Questions from Quartz

Use these questions for journaling, contemplation, or meditation; open your Akashic Records or the Akashic Records of Quartz and ask:

1. How can the clarity of Quartz help me find choice in the face of fear?
2. With Quartz, how can I shine light on the darkened corners of my life?
3. What message does Quartz have for me today about fear, clarity, and truth?
4. What is my personal relationship with the energy of Quartz?

2

AGATE
RAINBOW STRENGTH

An ornamental stone consisting of a hard variety of chalcedony, typically banded or otherwise variegated in color.

One of the prettiest necklaces I have received as a present is one composed of Agate. I don't remember the type, but I do remember the heft and beauty of the polished stones. Over the years, I have found that Agate can be easily overlooked in favor of other "sexy" gemstones like Amethyst or Tourmaline. That's a shame because this is a stone worthy of much admiration. Agate is serious support which has helped me see my own beauty.

We are a composite Guardianship. Across many forms and colors, our spiritual energy embraces physical manifestation on Earth.

Essentially, we are *chaord* – organized chaos focused on the expression of individual distinctions. Fluid in specific expression yet focused on supporting essential nature to step forward fully supported.

Instead of a focus on right or wrong, all Agate is focused on essential, authentic expression. *What calls to you?* This is our primary question for all expression in any moment.

Our soul story is soul expression – freely, openly, boundlessly. We are an aggregate which challenges preconceived notions of any sort. Yet we are connected, grounded, and in balance with the divine flow within the Earth plane.

In this period of massive Agreement shift, we are here to support individual experience and individual autonomy. There isn't right behavior. There is awareness and consciousness of connection of the divine inherent nature of all.

We observe disagreement is not the primary problem. Rather the issue is disagreement as justification for hate and fear, for choosing disconnection and rejection.

Fear is the primary interference to authentic expression and experience. Though humanity is no longer trapped in the hunt of predator and prey, this is the inherent habit which many are breaking.

The potential of the current global shift and an opportunity to embrace physical-spiritual integration empowers a new perspective and a new choice.

Passing from human experience is that all choice must be embedded in the structures of fear and the physical demands of safety. Especially those on Earth living outside of the physical threat of war have the opportunity to release centuries of habitual fear.

In the USA, for example, the war is psychological, emotional, and spiritual. Thus, to find physical-spiritual integration understand fear as a choice which need not be chosen to feel safe.

Those moving into physical-spiritual integration are re-aligning the body, mind, heart, and soul to a new understanding and experience of fear. Instead of feeling oppressed and unable to exercise personal choice, the energy of personal autonomy is being recognized and embraced.

Fear attempts to hide and denigrate personal power. As personal choice becomes more manageable and palatable, fear is released as a habitual reaction and an enforced choice.

Our message for humanity:

Find peace within to experience transcendence here, now.

Essentially, we are saying quit living like you have to wait until tomorrow to experience your greatness.

Putting off the best of you until later is nothing but an excuse. This is a clear refusal which is beneath you.

Live now. Today. In this moment.

Yes, tomorrow will be different. But this is never a reason to hold back.

Live now the best you can. Tomorrow you can adjust based on what you have learned. Tomorrow will happen one way or another. Best to be all of who you are than carry regret forever.

Remember:

Find peace within to experience transcendence here, now.

Personal Exploration Questions from Agate:

Use these questions for journaling, contemplation, or meditation; open your Akashic Records or the Akashic Records of Agate and ask:

1. How can I learn to be comfortable within chaos?
2. How do I keep myself from my best?
3. In what ways can I be more present in my life?
4. What is the soul message for me from Agate?

3

AMETHYST

PEACE IN BALANCE

Quartz of a violet or purple variety

Like many, Amethyst attracted me because of the beautiful color and its many variations. For many years, I had a very large piece sitting beside me in my office. She occupied a prime location because of the balance I felt. Just to glance or a quick touch and I could let go of resistance and the push of perfection. While many see Amethyst as a healing stone, my experience has always been more about release and balance. This experience has led me to understand much of the *how* of healing. For within the Akashic Records, healing is balance. And balance always is.

I am the guardian spirit of Amethyst. To you I will appear as one – a being of creation - a mother. But in truth, we Guardians of Amethyst stand in such a way that you only see and hear one.

In the beginning of all creation, we were part of the guardian energy of all creation. A guardian does not direct, a guardian holds safe space for energy to experience the flow of potential into form. As such we are also witness to the flow of creation. We inherently understand balance – and the necessity of balance for all creative endeavors. For restoration of balance – that which you call healing – this is a motion of balance.

At the origin of our soul energy is the desire to safeguard the balance of all creation, of all creative intent. We are of the whole, of divine source and of divine creation. In manifested form, we support the joy of wholeness and of balance.

While we are of a color because of chemical reactions during our forming phase, we are the color which brings a sense of restoration – balance – a guide toward the experience of wholeness. At origin, each soul is an experience of wholeness, oneness, boundlessness.

As Amethyst, we are the guardians of this original soul experience. Our primary intent is to hold space for all souls to experience soul wholeness. In manifested form this will often feel like a remembering or an uncovering. Though with learning and growth, our energy points into the possibilities of balance within new directions and new experiences. This feeling of balance and wholeness supports and encourages more learning and growth.

This is one of the fundamental concepts of physical-spiritual integration:

Learning fuels growth and release to expand the experience of physical-spiritual integration.

We are also here to help move beyond outdated beliefs of physical domination for there is no true balance when one aspect of existence dominates. This is not balance.

We fully support the infinite possibility of the dynamic view. For there is so much more possible on Earth if one will let go of the linear and the static. Within the dynamic, physical-spiritual integration moves into the boundlessness of experience. Within the dynamic, physical-spiritual expression is not a matter of how many dimensions. Rather, infinite opportunities for experiencing the continuum of All That Is from unity with the divine to full spiritual-physical integration within physical form. This is balance at an expanded level. We as guardians stand as witness and hold this space for the achievement of all humanity.

Our message for humanity:

Expansion is not in resistance but in the embrace of the unexpected.

There is a fear of losing control, of losing the ability to direct life. However, if human beings could learn anything from us it is about the connection between learning and the appearance of the unexpected. Learning brings forward the unexpected. The unexpected is not failure. Rather the unexpected is a clear indication of motion forward into the next phase of learning and growth. The unexpected appears because you are prepared, ready for the newness and its challenge. The unexpected is a step into deeper personal expansion and understanding.

Resistance comes when the unexpected is received in fear. Resistance isn't a sign of failure or of an inability to find your way. Instead, resistance is a sign to take a deep breath and ask:

How can I move through this opportunity which is raising fear and resistance?

What do I need to feel like I can thrive within this new situation?

Fear wants to turn everything into a threat to survival. This is a breakdown-fall-apart strategy.

Instead, Amethyst is breakthrough-to-new-balance energy.

Amethyst is the energy of new balance and a new awareness of wholeness. You do not need us physically in your presence to receive our energy. You need not even be aware for as the Guardians of Amethyst, we are with all humanity always. Physically in your presence, our energy is amplified. For the beginner, our physical presence helps connect to inner awareness of balance, of wholeness, and full restoration to their path of physical-spiritual integration.

Within the balance held by us, we can always support your desire to move forward in your life. Frustration and confusion will abate when you stop struggling to control anything around you.

The peace you seek comes through recognizing that the shift you so desperately desire is your ability to trust yourself to choose for yourself.

Peace does not come through guaranteed outcome or alliance with the "best expert." Peace does not come through winning by any means possible.

Peace in your heart comes by accepting your power within, by believing in your personal worth, and by realizing you owe no one an explanation to justify either your choice or your worth.

Remember:

Expansion is not in resistance but in the embrace of the unexpected.

Personal Exploration Questions from Amethyst:

Use these questions for journaling, contemplation, or meditation; open your Akashic Records or the Akashic Records of Amethyst and ask:

1. When am I most likely to blame myself for failure? Blame others?
2. How am I afraid of peace in my heart?
3. How can I feel the balance of me?
4. What is the energy of Amethyst for me?

4

CARNELIAN
MYSTERY REVEALS

A deep red or brownish pink form of Chalcedony.
From the Latin meaning flesh-colored.

This is a stone at the edge of my experience. A peace and a sense of quiet. Yet an ancient strength similar to Ancient Mother. A witness and a guardian at the gate of my experience. No need to be attached to me to be connected. No need to sit beside me. Yet always there, guiding, holding me safe.

We greet you with joy in our hearts and wish you the feeling of peace and alignment. We come forward as envoys of balance and alignment. We come forward as reminders of the joy you can feel when you are at peace and no longer jerked by the vagaries of fear.

Our soul energy is of this alignment and of this joy. Our soul intention is to show you how to open your heart to yourself. How to provide your heart protection without the need to silence it.

Protection is an interesting motion seen from an energetic perspective. To protect is to show honor and respect to boundary – boundary being the discernment of what is you and your responsibility. Often protection is cast beyond personal boundary.

Protection is also a necessity when body, mind, heart, and soul are experienced as divided, separated from one another. In this separation, is a sense of disconnection, of being one against the unconquerable horde of danger.

When body, mind, heart, and soul are lost within the onslaught to survive no matter the cost, the separation is no longer experienced as a challenge. Rather the division is considered normal human experience.

Our message for humanity are words to ignite the claiming of your entirety of being, your fullness, wholeness, and infinite possibility.

This is for you to remember, to believe in yourself, in your full experience as beings of light and sound.

Like humanity, Carnelian is a gemstone in great transition. Our original form was very much a replication of the blood of the human body.

We came forward just in this incarnation of Earth as support for the physical strength of the body as the integration of the physical with the spiritual continues its deep path of recovery and restoration.

We are also here to help anchor deeper conscious awareness within a physical body that for the most part was created to resist deep consciousness.

Our message for humanity:

Your heart lights your path.
Your body is a fountain of wisdom.
Your mind connects with the boundlessness of the
infinite and the eternal.
Your soul is your unique expression of divine source.

In this transition, Carnelian is leading the awareness of body, mind, heart, and soul into a remembering and a claiming. There is not a natural division within you. Instead, you are whole, connected, undivided.

This is why our message is what it is – guidance for recovering what has been lost. Support for attempting integration. Words of memory lost, now ready to be retrieved.

To reclaim your wholeness remember who you are: a being of light and sound capable of miracles and unknown acts of kindness.

There is always more than you can imagine.

This is not a matter of intimidation.

This is real life: possibility always exists in every moment of your life. Your choice guides your journey. The circumstances may not be to your liking. Yet, choice is always yours.

Your body, mind, heart, and soul are fully present to you and for you.

Your life's journey weaves your cloth of destiny on a journey which never ends.

Don't try to understand the mysteries by holding back. Only by taking this step does experience reveal the unknown.

There is much love for you always! Journey in peace and joy!

Remember:

Your heart lights your path.
Your body is a fountain of wisdom.
Your mind connects with the boundlessness of the infinite and the eternal.
Your soul is your unique expression of divine source.

Personal Exploration Questions from Carnelian:

Use these questions for journaling, contemplation, or meditation; open your Akashic Records or the Akashic Records of Carnelian and ask:

1. How can I feel at ease when the mysteries of the universe are revealed to me?
2. What steps can I take to honor myself and my life's journey?
3. What are the mysteries of my body, mind, heart, and soul?
4. What is the energy of Carnelian for me?

5

CELESTITE

CELESTIAL WALKER

A mineral of sulphate and strontium named for its typical sky-blue color. From the Latin celeste, *sky-blue.*

Celestite is one of the newest gemstones in my life. The Guardians suggested her as I began work for this book. I find a lack of struggle and space to be. A kindred soul at peace with the future however it may appear. Celestial Walker's presence encourages me to step into the celestial wonders with curiosity and excitement.

Like Rose Quartz, or Heart Crystal Quartz, we have our own inner spirit name: Celestial Walker.

Our energy is about moving beyond limitation, especially physical boundary, and venturing into the celestial heavens to see beyond.

To confront fear of the unknown and to see inner capacity in a new light.

To see your spiritual expression is not bound by your physical being.

We as the gemstone, Celestial Walker, are energetic expression of deep and profound exploration of the world and of the dynamic possibilities of the infinite and eternal.

Our soul energy is expansive and creative. We are joyful in the broad view of the multi-dimensional expressions of All That Is. Our energy supports connection and interaction with this broad, unlimited view.

In the boundlessness is a clarity of all which is accessible when you are not bound by fear.

Only the choice of fear limits. Only the choice of limitation cuts you off from your inherent capacity, available always.

This perspective is how we endeavor to support your motion within the new Earth energies and agreements of physical-spiritual integration.

We intend that our presence creates the environment for integration and any possible transformation or transmutation to occur in a natural process – a process of joy and connection rather than habitual retreat in fear.

We believe when fear can be consciously stepped away from, awareness of balance moves forward naturally.

Essentially fear hides awareness, especially awareness of balance.

Our message for humanity:

Because fear is about choice, in any moment you can choose balance, peace, and joy.

If you can begin to see fear as that which is pushed at you to bind and create a false perception of limitation, then you can begin to free yourself to respond differently to the external push with a new, integrated pattern born of personal strength and power within.

Remember, life is not about completely ridding self of patterns or habits.

Instead, life is about shifting from unconscious effort and reaction to the conscious choice of how you express self and choose to experience life.

Choice itself is a pattern and a habit.

As you move away from the manipulation of the world outside and the unconscious deferral to its authority, the conscious habit of your power within can move forward.

Your power within is your fuel. Your power within is the center of your conscious choice and empowers you to release all which no longer serves your being and becoming.

Your power within also maintains the awareness of when shift away from habits and patterns serves the truth of your highest expression. Your power within is not bound to yesterday's truth. Instead, your power within is of you in this moment, honoring your autonomy, your self-determination, and your self-worth.

While balance always is, where the truth of your balance is in this moment may not be the same as previous moments or future moments.

Coming from the conscious awareness of balance in the present moment, your power within can guide you to self-truth, joy, and peace.

Your power within is not separate from you. Your power within is you fully conscious, willing to accept responsibility for you and your life, willing to entertain the ambiguities, challenges, and infinite possibilities of life.

Yet the choice of fear can disrupt belief in the appropriateness of the power within and the truth of self – especially a self consciously choosing life within physical-spiritual integration.

Fear wants to convince that perfection and rightness are required to experience profound levels of spiritual expression. Fear challenges your sense of physical safety.

Fear maintains that the physical and the spiritual are separate, feeble, and unworthy as expressed within you. Fear aims to cripple your ability to choose for yourself and to trust yourself.

Dynamically beyond the limitations of a static, linear view, there is not separation. Instead, there is connection felt both locally and nonlocally.

Moving beyond horizontal and vertical, both physical and

spiritual are expressions of the infinite and eternal aspects of your soul.

Your unique expression as you connected always with All That Is.

Get this today: There is no separation. There is no division. Instead, there is connection across all dimensions local and non-local.

We, like you, are Celestial Walkers across the infinite and eternal. We call to you and entreat you to begin to shift your awareness and response to fear.

We are here to support you now and always.

Remember:

Because fear is about choice, in any moment you can choose balance, peace, and joy.

Personal Exploration Questions from Celestite:

Use these questions for journaling, contemplation, or meditation; open your Akashic Records or the Akashic Records of Celestite and ask:

1. How can I become more aware of the presence of fear in my body, mind, heart, and soul?
2. How can I develop more trust in myself?
3. What habits or patterns no longer serve me?
4. What is the energy of Celestite or Celestial Walker for me?

6

CHALCEDONY
COLLECTED ORIGINS

A cryptocrystalline form of quartz, having a waxy lustre, and being either transparent or translucent.

This is another stone which is brand new to me with this work. Yet one I have already found worthy of inclusion. There is an ancient foundation which helps me connect with the primordial and the origin both within me and within All That Is. I am reminded that there is more than we can contemplate beyond us. More than we can experience in a million lifetimes. And yet, we try. We return again and again. To take in the miraculous in this breath, in this grain of sand, in this sun ray from above.

. . .

W ithin us, there is much to understand energetically. One perspective is about the difference between an individual point of view and a collective perspective.

Embedded in its motion, energy has the capacity to filter multiple layers or dimensions of knowing. In other words, we speak of motion within knowing. This motion is guided by intention and is a feedback loop, an interactive exchange between all layers or dimensions. Intention is guided by knowing.

Energy has within itself both the tools and the capacity for self-awareness and may be turned in any direction of knowing. Energy's self-awareness is self-propagated, arising from within according to its own sense of direction and intention. Energy is fueled from within.

If everything is energy – and we believe this both as fact and as our experience – then, like everything, humanity is energy. Thus, human awareness is not created externally. Awareness arises within from their internal sense of motion, intention, and knowing. Awareness is created within. Awareness then can be turned in any direction within and explore the infinite and eternal layers of expression contained within self's motion, intention, and knowing.

This is a long way of saying that our soul's mission as Chalcedony is to support the infinite layers of human awareness. Our support comes in essentially two forms: individual and collective. By doing this, we are supporting the individual's inner connection with the awareness of self.

Plus, we support the individual's foray into non-local dynamic awareness and connection which forms the basis of inter-dimensional awareness and connection. Both horizontal and vertical awareness if you will.

Our support comes from within our own collective experience of inter-dimensional and unified connection and exchange. We are manifested on Earth now for this purpose.

The time has come within the experience of Earth's humanity to begin to access the multi-dimensional aspects of All That Is. This is why your agreements are shifting. To move forward, humans must shift their awareness away from separation and turn inner awareness toward the infinite possibility of multi-dimensionality.

Unlike the faulty assumptions which pervade human religion and politics, humanity is infinitely capable of multiple levels of awareness all contained within the perspectives of either local or non-local. For these are not lines or directions – rather infinite dimensions spreading out into the outer reaches and the inner depths.

Physically, this appears more like a pinpoint radiating in all directions creating an infinite sphere of motion, intention, and knowing. For each soul is this infinite and eternal energetic expression forever radiating from source.

Chalcedony holds the energy and the awareness of the radiating soul. With clear awareness, the soul traverses the inherent multi-dimensionality of All That Is. Our presence on Earth creates and supports the possibility of awakening to this intrinsic, eternal connection within.

We, thus, support each person's power within as internal focus of self-awareness, self-responsibility, and self-propagating experience and choice.

Our message for humanity:

Life is for all who dare to live in the fullness of infinite possibility.

To live fully, freely, beyond fear requires you to dance life in the light of infinite possibility. This is a dance which radiates from the powerful center of who you are and who you dare in each moment to become.

Being and becoming are not separate experiences. Like all energy, being and becoming arise from the awareness of your motion, intention, and knowing. Chalcedony is the energy of being and becoming –we are experts, well-versed guides of the journey from this moment to all moments.

What does it mean to dare? This means that you don't hold yourself back because of fear or because of past experience. To dare is to step into the next moment of your life without assurance of outcome. To dare is to dance with infinite possibility so that your being blooms into your becoming.

You are the infinite, radiating expression of your soul forever capable of dancing in the multi-dimensional aspects of All That Is.

In this dance, each moment is a dare to live in the fullness of your being and in the infinite blooming of your becoming. With our presence and within your own awareness, you can dare all.

Remember:

Life is for all who dare to live in the fullness of infinite possibility.

Personal Exploration Questions from Chalcedony:

Use these questions for journaling, contemplation, or meditation; open your Akashic Records or the Akashic Records of Chalcedony and ask:

1. What holds me back from daring all?
2. How can I live from the center of infinite awareness within me?
3. How am I connected with multi-dimensionality? How can I make this awareness part of my everyday life?
4. What is my personal connection with Chalcedony?

7

CITRINE

SOUL LIGHT

A yellow form of quartz typically colored by the presence of iron.
A borrowing from Latin and French for yellow.

Citrine feels full of sunshine – a clear light of love and support. Like Rose Quartz/Heart Crystal Quartz, Citrine is at the edge of my awareness lighting the darkened corners. Citrine is reliable and supportive. Present. Showing me how my being can also be present, reliable, and illuminated from within.

We, Citrine, have a very specific intention: support clarity.

We don't just mean mental clarity – though this is extremely important. We are connected to the support of spiritual clarity. A clarity of the soul and how it expresses as manifested being.

More importantly, we support the clarity which comes in integration. The clarity available as one overcomes separation and begins to live within the unity of connection.

This doesn't mean to give up self. No. Awareness of connection comes in the deepest awareness. Clarity is intrinsic to you no matter the other conditions or experiences of your life.

The challenge is that some clarity is not pleasant. Some clarity excites pain. Some clarity exacerbates awareness of what resists acknowledgment in the moment.

If instead you engage with clarity as that which assists in moving through what no longer serves, you will experience a new perspective.

Clarity supports release. Clarity supports the integration. Clarity is the *A-ha!* moment when energy shifts into the balance of the moment.

Whatever clarity brings forward, it does so because your foundation is firm enough to support the new perspective. Clarity strengthens integration and strengthens body, mind, heart, and soul to absorb and reflect the new awareness of inner strength and power within.

Clarity creates awareness of the inherent potential and mastery of your personal power.

Clarity shines on love. Clarity shines as love.

The firm motion of knowing and learning claims clarity. Empowered, strengthened, and worthy, clarity is welcome to shine understanding and presence on you, for you.

Just a thought on us is enough to help you step into clear, balanced, resonant clarity. We are present always!

Our message for humanity:

Feel your light shine from within.

There is always the possibility of light within your life. Sometimes you can only see a glimmer, a tiny sliver of what is real and available.

In our energy is the encouragement to slowly find a way to live within the awareness of your light and within the awareness of how all manifested creation is of the light.

Even the dark corners and the unlit connections are of the light. Exactly how has not been revealed to you yet.

Trust and the connections will be revealed.

Remember:

Feel your light shine from within.

Personal Exploration Questions from Citrine:

Use these questions for journaling, contemplation, or meditation; open your Akashic Records or the Akashic Records of Citrine and ask:

1. What clouds my heart and my mind?
2. How can I experience a fully integrated, firm foundation?
3. How does my soul express through clarity?
4. What is the truth of Citrine for me?

8

COPPER
CONDUCTIVE SPIRIT

Distinguished by its particular red color, a metal of the Periodic Table, which is malleable, strong, and can be hammered or flattened.

For me, Copper begins with color. The burnished red is beautiful. However, it's not the red which introduced me to Copper. The introduction came when I was about ten and my Father was explaining the meaning of the word *verdigris*. Sometimes metal reacts with air and a new substance is formed, he told me. Holding out an old piece of copper wire and pointing to the blue-green stuff on the wire, this is *verdigris* he explained. I asked if you could make more if you blew on the wire. No, he said, the *verdigris* emerges over time. Which is what Copper has done:

emerged in my life over time and often in moments where I need to let go and move on. Now I dream of a copper-covered writing table.

The energy of Copper is ancient and foundational to the activity and aesthetics of humanity.

As you know, our energy is conductive and activating. A motion across, through, by, and with. We provide a foundation for creative motion. We fuel creative action.

We hold the action of heart beat safe, steady, wholly functional. For we, Copper, do literally support the human heartbeat on all levels, physical and spiritual.

The heartbeat is the rhythm of life. Its cadence in tune with the heartbeat of All That Is.

The heartbeat is of the Eternal Return. Like breath, a motion followed by a moment of stillness, then a return to motion.

Copper holds the space for both the motion and the stillness. Without either and without the orchestration of the entirety of the beat, there would be no human life. For the heartbeat is integral to the motion of breath.

Copper then is both beat and breath.

While you may not be aware of its importance within, even the smallest amount around you, especially wire fashioned into a spiral, is potent reminder and active conductor of the heartbeat of your life.

Our message for humanity:

Breathe.
Dance in balance with your beat.
Experience life in a state of awe.

Heartbeat is balance, is return, is acknowledgment that life moves, continues, and returns.

Heartbeat is the foundation of trust. Thus, the presence of Copper reinforces trust and self-belief.

The heartbeat of your personal power within is Copper as you capable within this beat and the next. Copper fuels your power and activates the unique cadence which is you. As conductor, Copper energizes the state of energy transported from one still point to another.

When conduction is faulty, that which does not move from one point to another as intended will be frozen and its motion incomplete. Thus, conductive, the flow of your energy plus how you interact and connect with your surroundings is supported by your heartbeat and Copper.

Your life rests in the simplicity of the beat and of the stillness.

Copper follows intention and supports completed motion within any and all flows of energy both physical and spiritual.

Again through conduction, Copper follows and supports the motion of intention as it shifts, transforms, and transmutes within both the spiritual and the physical experience.

The presence of Copper supports the energetic phases humans experience as learning, expansion, and healing. Copper is always present to balance, to truth, to the soul's deepest, healthiest expression. Copper is the energy of awe, of wonder, of amazement.

This is the energy present to and conductive of the spark of life which fills both beat and breath.

Your capacity is to be present to both beat and breath. In this awareness is alignment and resonance with divine balance and divine pulse. Hold a small piece of Copper to your heart and feel you and how you are always connected to the divine pulse of All That Is.

Make of me not a ring but a coil or a spiral, as symbol of that which eternally returns: your heart, your breath, your awe-filled life.

Know there is naught but connection. There is naught but joy in the experience of divinely connected awe.

Remember:

Breathe.
Dance in balance with your beat.
Experience life in a state of awe.

Personal Exploration Questions from Copper:

Use these questions for journaling, contemplation, or meditation; open your Akashic Records or the Akashic Records of Copper and ask:

1. How do I limit the fullness of my breath?
2. How can I expand my awareness of the balance of me?
3. How can Copper help me become aware within the still point?
4. What is the energy of Copper for me?

9

FLUORITE

SIMPLY CLARITY

A calcium fluoride mineral as cubic or octahendral crystals,
typically colorless though also colored through impurities.

Like Obsidian, my experience with Fluorite began with absorption. Fluorite showed me how negative, traumatic, draining energy can be absorbed simply by holding a piece in my hand. At first, I was skeptical. But I tried. I was down and feeling miserable as I released the accumulated muck of my life. I realized Fluorite used refracted light through its cells to absorb the muck. When I set the Fluorite in sunlight, the muck was released in the sun rays. I learned I could let go safely within the light.

. . .

F luorite responds to the integration of body and heart.

Fluorite brings together the sense of thought and the sense of feeling into balance within a united whole. This union assists the human being to respond and live life from this balance and this integration.

Fluorite has been on Earth since the beginning of Earth's physical expression and has always been an important component in establishing clear human expression.

Previous to the emergence of human activity on Earth, Fluorite was an important gemstone expression for clarity. Fluorite can clear impurities out of the atmosphere and remove energy which is harmful, challenging, or threatening to all physical bodies, human, animal, or otherwise.

Fluorite sees all expressions with a heartbeat as variations of the same type of energetic expression.

With a focus on the body and the heart, there is a very important balance to be found between what is physical and what is spiritual.

Over time Fluorite has become more important to human expression because of its ability to create open pathways or channels between the heart and the physical body.

Humanity is moving toward a greater alignment with nature. This brings forward a deeper sense of balance and connection with nature.

Fluorite supports spiritual balance and physical balance both and especially supports the integration between both.

Our message for humanity:

Simply ... Live.

There's much in the environment which seems to complicate life's pure expression of balance. However, this complication is truly about fear and the misuse of power.

If Fluorite could have anything clearly understood, it would be the nature of fear as an illusion to manipulate and control.

When there is balance within, between body and heart, mind and soul, there is a clarity which rises above the motion of fear and responds with clarity, compassion, and love.

Fluorite held in the hand or set beside a workplace will lend itself towards clearing the surrounding environment. Within this clearing, you can feel into the depths of yourself with a compassionate clarity which helps you identify what can be let go, what no longer serves, and how to move forward with confidence and a clear sense of self-worth.

Remember:

Simply ... Live.

Personal Exploration Questions from Fluorite:

Use these questions for journaling, contemplation, or meditation; open your Akashic Records or the Akashic Records of Fluorite and ask:

1. What steps can I take to simplify my life?
2. How do I create my own complications?
3. What needs clearing within me?
4. What is the energy of Fluorite for me?

10

GARNET
SOUL WITNESS

A deep transparent red mineral in a glassy crystal form.

Just after I divorced, I came across a jewelry maker at a summer street fair who had made a beautiful necklace of Garnet. I tried to walk away. I tried to ignore Garnet's pull on me. I tried to pretend as if there was no connection. I wanted to pretend I didn't need assistance or support. Well, long story short, the necklace and matching earrings came home with me. After a day or so, I knew I had made a great choice because I felt an incredible joy wearing the necklace. I felt a warmth within me that had been missing for a while. I felt a strength well up within me. The set is still with me and every now and then I put them on just cause.

. . .

L ike our physical manifestation, Garnet is the powerful energy of heated extrusion.

There is incredible strength which comes from this pressured process.

There is also resilience. Resilience is the foundation of Garnet.

Garnet is also one of the older gemstones having evolved in Earth's first expression sometime after Quartz.

Though where Quartz is a pressurized crystalline structure, Garnet is a smooth heated extrusion.

If Garnet were a person, Garnet would sit to the edge of a group and observe, able to understand the immediate connections or disconnections within the group.

Garnet observes all, witnesses all, and takes in all.

Garnet then helps solidify experience into the strength needed to stand up against fear and a lack of intention.

For within its resilience, Garnet it the intention to make choices from the clarity and the resilience of truth and the authenticity of physical expression.

Our primary support of physical-spiritual integration is through the concept of resilience.

That's where we find our spiritual balance and that is where we are able to support humanity.

. . .

Our message for humanity is:

Move from survive to thrive.

Resiliency cannot be maintained if you are stuck in the fear of survival.

If you have moved to the place where you feel connection within yourself and with All That Is, you are moving into the energy that comes through physical-spiritual integration.

This is the energy to thrive.

Resilience is thriving, thriving is resilience – or at least thriving is difficult if you do not understand within yourself how to be resilient.

To be resilient means that you don't turn away from the unexpected or from stress or danger.

Instead, give yourself a chance to understand what you can do and how you can respond.

By learning to embrace the concept of resiliency, humanity can move forward because spiritual-physical integration is the foundation for resilience.

Remember:

Move from survive to thrive.

Personal Exploration Questions from Garnet:

Use these questions for journaling, contemplation, or meditation; open your Akashic Records or the Akashic Records of Garnet and ask:

1. How can I move more fully from survive to thrive?
2. In a group, how can I be more witness than judge?
3. What steps can I take to expand my resiliency?
4. What is the energy of Garnet for me?

11

GRANITE
SOLID FOUNDATION

A granular crystalline rock consisting essentially of quartz, feldspar, and mica.

As I wrote my first book, every day was an amazing experience which also had its moments of distraction. Not only did I spend hours in the Akashic Records in deep conversation, within my writing process I often lost awareness of my desk and my room. I was entirely focused on encouraging the words to appear on to the blank page before me. The process often left me with the feeling that my head was dragging across the ceiling in not a good way. I was concentrated on the work, yet a bit untethered within the energy. I asked my Akashic Records for suggestions. Their quick response: Granite. I did as they suggested and found four large pieces of granite and put one in each of the four corners of my office. Overnight, I went from untethered to fully present and highly focused and absorbed. No longer feeling like I was floating off, I felt reigned in and present, yet, still able to produce a huge volume of organized thought and awareness. Yes, the Granite was grounding – but more than the grounding was the sense of being clearly focused. Now when I begin in a new space, I bring in the energy of Granite and rely on its presence to support my presence.

We, as Granite, feel in alignment with humanity because we too are a physical aggregate of the Earth plane. As such our energy is one of grounding, of solid structure, and of a love for the foundation of all physical energy.

Our soul story begins in the physical development history of Earth. From her first incarnation, Earth has been an environment for creation. This is a creation which emerges from the integration of multiple flows of energy. Then this creative motion utilizes other energy flows to transform and transmute the essential nature of the first phase of creation.

Erosion, pressure, heat, and cold are just a few of these creative processes. Each interacts with the elements and energies of Earth to create, to transform, and to transmute.

Granite is an energy of transmutation where origin elements shift into something beyond where we began.

This shift in our essential nature is a powerful process of becoming through synthesis and transmutation. Similar to the arising of the Phoenix. Life is the same but forever transformed.

We can also talk about this as a process of being and becoming. In the first step is the awareness of *What Is* in this moment. A clarity of the parts and the present flows. The next step is the experience of life – a process of choice and engagement which begins the feedback loop which is present within any interaction. The observer and the observed – of flow and exchange where there is fluidity and the observed becomes observer in the flow. Rigidity occurs when there is resistance to the natural exchange inherent in this experience of life.

Resistance is most often powered by fear. Fear comes naturally within this exchange which skirts or dives into the unknown. Fear of the unknown, while slowly abating within human awareness, has been a significant influence on human life in the last 2000 to 3000 years. This is why fear can also be employed as a tool of manipulation or coercion.

Fear can stop independent, creative action, and personal choice. Fear attempts to hide possibility and demonize the unknown. Fear creates blame, shame, and disconnection.

Returning to the exchange of observed and observer, each can make the choice to step beyond the limits of fear. This offers the opportunity to step into the creative process beyond the resistance asserted by fear. The being dares to challenge self. The being begins a dance within the unknown possibility where life might take an unexpected direction or engage in an unanticipated interaction with the creative forces of life.

Pressure moves towards synthesis. Erosion empowers release. Heat bakes the body, mind, heart, and soul while cold both expands and contracts.

Together the creative forces brew a new expression of the primary elements as what is no longer needed is released, transformed, or transmuted. *What Is* shifts to becoming. Being no longer resists new possibility.

Maybe this is not the picture of Granite which is common. However, energetically, Granite is focused on the dance of life and assisting life to be grounded in reality while also being able to interact and be transformed by the opportunity of the unknown.

Our message for humanity:

Choosing fear defeats the purpose of life.
Choosing the unknown of life claims the best you can be and become.

We see that much of humanity has let go, has become passive and reactive, preferring blame, shame, and fear. This is a choice which can be reversed by making a different choice.

When you choose to accept the observer-observed dance inherent in life, then you are making the choice to embrace the creative forces of life which will hone your awareness to a sharp and clear vista. From this perspective, possibility is apparent even if only for a moment. You are now able to sense the calling of your tomorrow before today is complete.

You see and respond to the creative forces as a natural part of life's processes. You are not in resistance – or you are able to feel and sense resistance. Looking resistance square on means you are able to do your work and release whatever is standing in your way of realizing your being and claiming your becoming.

Beware of those who attempt distraction. Know your path can always be regained no matter the duration or depth of the distraction.

Beware those who incite fear especially with denigrating labels and outright slander. Just as you do, all people are deserving of direct connection and respect. There is nothing respectful in stuffing people into faux groupings and slapping on labels meant to demean and control.

Each person is exactly that: a person. Deal with each individual as the amazing person that they are. Eliminate labels in your thoughts and in your beliefs. The associated fears will fade when you acknowledge the amazing humanity of each person.

Ultimately, Granite is here to support your Phoenix nature – your ability to emerge from the creative fires as a powerful expression of Eternal Source. See us with the same capacity and know the depth of your creative nature will always make it through the transmutative energies of life as authentic, real, and complete.

Remember:

Choosing fear defeats the purpose of life.
Choosing the unknown of life claims the best you can be and become.

Personal Exploration Questions from Granite:

Use these questions for journaling, contemplation, or meditation; open your Akashic Records or the Akashic Records of Granite and ask:

1. How can I trust myself to be and become my true self?
2. What steps can I take to become less wary of the unknown?
3. What makes me choose fear?
4. What is the energy of Granite for me?

12

HEMATITE
FLUID SOLID

An abundant and widely distributed iron ore, occurring in various forms (crystalline, massive, or granular); in color, red, reddish-brown, or blackish with a red streak. From the Latin, literally stone of blood.

Until I began this work with the Gemstone Guardians, I did not have a relationship with Hematite. Yet as I learned, the energy of this Gemstone has shown me a new path of understanding – both of me and of Hematite. A work in progress for both of us. A willingness to learn and a willingness to share. We both will continue turning corners and finding new perspectives on this incredible life we share.

. . .

We want first to say that our energy is different from most Gemstones. Our energy is of a fluid solid rather than a fluid spirit (like Amethyst or Citrine, for example).

This is because we are entirely of the Earth plane in this incarnation and share similar characteristics with liquid mercury and liquid silver.

First understand our physical expression: we emerged through the guidance of Ancient Mother, the spiritual progenitor of all physical expression on Earth. She called us forward from the primordial form of Earth to assist in physical expression.

Our creation beat in time with Earth's emergence reflecting a new expression – or at least new aspects to Earth's current physical expression.

In a sense, we are primarily physical expression. A solid, physical creation reflecting the physicality of Earth, here, now.

The current expression of Earth reflects a capacity for flexibility. An ebb and flow which is able to shift and adjust as the conditions and foundation adapt to circumstances. Earth in her current incarnation is all about flexibility and adaptability to allow and provide the same to all who choose incarnation within her sphere of support.

We, as Hematite, found physical expression within this flexibility. We can adapt easily without needing to lose our physical form.

This flexible capacity is exactly what humanity needs. Especially now, as the entirety of the essence of humanity is radically shifting.

For the shift is happening and will continue over the next fifty to one hundred years. No matter how much you might try, you cannot put the brakes on this global and inter-dimensional shift.

This world, your life, is held within an unstoppable motion. You can either go through this kicking and screaming in denial. Or you can learn flexibility and adaptability.

That's our message for humanity:

Resist or Receive – your choice!

The good news is that you do have choice. You may not always like the presented choice. However, we believe that if you will realize two seemingly contrary concepts, you can live your life with clarity and self-respect.

First, as you move forward, life is in the awareness of what moves toward you easily and freely. Becoming adaptable is consciously taking self out of the unending rat race wheel where personal motion is consumed in running after, never catching the carrot or reaching an assumed destination.

Second, because your worth is inherent, neither adaptability nor flexibility are signs of weakness or self-denial. Instead, both are motions away from the incessant demand to know or to be right.

Motions toward learning to be comfortable not knowing or

feeling like you must always be able to explain why anything happens in your life.

This is not to say you can't or shouldn't want to know why. Instead, it's a release of the insidious demand that your mind always be able to explain why.

When you are comfortable with *I don't know,* you are able to reside in the ease of flexibility and adaptability.

Now give yourself the space to be aware of what moves toward you freely and easily.

In a moment existing beyond expectation and demand, understanding moves into your awareness. Destination becomes process and you live life with a new-found grace and ease.

Hematite is both reminder and supporter for you as your life shifts and you receive new perspectives and new understanding.

Life now provides solid foundation to your trust and your truth!

Remember:

Resist or Receive – your choice!

Personal Exploration Questions from Hematite:

Use these questions for journaling, contemplation, or

meditation; open your Akashic Records or the Akashic Records of Hematite and ask:

1. How can I learn to be gracefully flexible in my life?
2. What is the source of believing I am not worthy enough?
3. How can I learn living is a process rather than a string of destinations?
4. What is my personal relationship with Hematite?

13

JASPER
ANCIENT UNITY

A variety of crystalline quartz, usually red, yellow, or brown in color due to the presence of iron oxide.

When I was about six, I was with my family and grandparents in Utah near the Four Corners area. We were walking and exploring the area where we stopped for a picnic. I found this beautiful reddish stone and showed it to my grandfather. What is it, I asked. His answer: Jasper. I laughed and told him that I wanted to know about the stone not him. His name was Jasper. You were named after a stone, I asked. No, he replied, the stone was named after me! Thus, for me, Jasper is my grandfather and this incredible stone of connection and solid presence. Both have been with me for most of my life.

. . .

We are pleased to share our story with you. We hold ancient Earth energy. Traces of primordial beginnings. Traces of both terrestrial and non-terrestrial. We hold this energy both as reminder and as opportunity for creating new frameworks for physical existence.

Our energy is quiet and reserved for a reason: the uniting of ancient motion with future possibility is not for those who are faint of heart, in resistance, or in denial.

To bring forward truth both within ancient expression and future capacity requires the ability to avoid mindless reaction, the quiet approach of equanimity, the peace of balance.

As energetic support, we hold attention to the awareness and expression of balance within even when there is turmoil without.

We focus on concentration. We hold the space for mindful absorption where inner awareness is guide rather than the coercion of external forces.

To be able to mindfully respond requires inner strength built intentionally within the challenges of life. Also required is belief in the inherent sense of trust and truth.

External forces work diligently to undermine this uniquely important self-belief. This self-belief is intrinsic to each person but is always held suspect by external forces which cannot succeed if people trust themselves.

Ancient Earth energy is both origin and container for intrinsic human value. We, as Jasper, act as conduit to humanity for this energy.

We also stand as conduit for the incoming energy which is in alignment with a future of physical-spiritual integration. An integration which has not been fully experienced by humanity in 2000 to 3000 years.

Jasper is here, now, to stand at the apex of this connection and support growing awareness of this opportunity and this connection between ancient expression and future possibility.

Our message for humanity:

Within the balance of Being, the connection of ancient expression with future possibility is the experience of today and your soul's path for tomorrow.

What needs to be left behind is not ancient expression.

Rather, jettison the disbelief in self-worth perpetuated by those external forces seeking always to control you and dictate and limit personal choice and self-belief.

Rejecting your true essence is that which is sought. Claiming your true essence is what we as Jasper can support you to and through.

Essence and its truth is held with this breath now. Focus on your breath and, with practice, you can begin to sense resistance and disdain of your worth and essence.

Little by little, you can begin to unveil your true essence to yourself, like removing the tarnish from your grandmother's silver spoon.

Uncovering reveals the shine, the light of your being's true essence and the balance of you, here, now, body, mind, heart, and soul.

You, able to commune with your true essence, is part of your power within stepping forward not in coercive control but within and from your center of true essence.

Jasper patiently exists within true essence as guide and lighthouse for you to live your life guided by the authenticity of your true essence.

True essence is light which can be dimmed but never extinguished.

Jasper light reflects your light. Let yourself shine!

Remember:

Within the balance of Being, the connection of ancient expression with future possibility is the experience of today and your soul's path for tomorrow.

Personal Exploration Questions from Jasper:

Use these questions for journaling, contemplation, or meditation; open your Akashic Records or the Akashic Records of Jasper and ask:

1. How do I ignore or deny my true essence, my inner light?
2. What can I do today or tomorrow which I feared I couldn't do yesterday?
3. How can I consciously connect my ancient expression and my future possibility?
4. What is my personal relationship with Jasper?

14

LABRADORITE
ANCHOR OF LIGHT

A feldspar mineral typically grayish-white in color, sometimes with blue iridescence occurring in both igneous and metamorphic rock. First found in Labrador.

Following a strong insistence to go in, I met Labradorite on a shelf in a store. I'd never really paid attention to this stone before but in that moment, I heard a strong message. *Take me home.* I turned away for a moment and swore I heard a very dignified harumph. I looked back. *You need me right now to weather your parting.* I turned away again, hearing a deep sigh. I was at the very beginning stages of divorce and feeling a bit tender on the edges. What good was a rock for that experience? But as I scanned the store, nothing else caught my attention and I realized I did want to return to the Labradorite. No more conversation. Transaction completed, home we went. A day or so went by and I realized I forgotten to retrieve my Labradorite from my purse. Now the insistence was placement. *On your desk please.* Why? *You'll see.* And I did. Over the next couple of months, the energy of parting was absorbed by the Labradorite. Whether it was anger or tears or hair strands, the energy was siphoned off and held in safety for me. For me Labradorite is about restoring peace after broken connection. Thank you!

We are the Guardians of Labradorite.

Our souls' story has to do with the way light as energy can be harnessed within the physical form to benefit forward motion.

When you become consciously aware of the light that is you, you are able to feel a connection to All That Is which assists transcending the worries and the concerns of life.

We emerged within a bath of darkness as ten points of light joined and connected. Physically, our forms can be both rough and smooth on the surface. However, the way we have melded together is the important element: layer upon layer of light with various elements joining together to maintain light within a bath of darkness.

Yes, we are fired in heat – yet we use that heat to generate and maintain the light.

This is a lesson for all mankind. Within each person, within each being, within each expression of energy flow is the possibility of connected light.

There's no reason to be afraid because there is joy to be had in understanding that the world is one of connection rather than disconnection.

By taking in our story and all the stories of all the Guardians, you can see and feel that connection exists within you. This is what we want you to understand.

Our energy, like yours, is relevant to all other forms of expression on the planet.

There are differences and similarities in connection. For example, the way we connect with horses is different than the way we connect with human beings. And we connect with both just as you can connect with us and with other energetic or physical expressions.

Maybe the connection will come and go. Be different in one moment compared to another. This is just the nature of connection.

Light itself shifts and with it connection shifts.

We are here to help with feeling that connection to light.

We know that feeling connected to light takes time. Time is needed to keep from wanting to immediately put up limitations or to turn away.

Labradorite is also very much wanting to support the transition for humanity into physical-spiritual integration.

We know that each person has their path and their pace that they need to take to feel the integration as a positive experience.

For many, this integrative process can be too challenging or too frightening.

In understanding, we stand as witness and will move forward when you reach out and feel an urge to connect with us.

We will force no one because that is absolutely the motion that humanity is moving away from. Moving away from the reactions of fear and blame, you are moving into an expression of wonder and awe.

Our point of spiritual balance comes in the awareness that light and dark are not divisions but are both expressions of divine knowing.

Our message for humanity:

Growth comes in the light and in the dark, and in the known and in the unknown.

What was unknowable yesterday always has the potential to be known today.

Given this possibility, we can help humanity move forward by providing an anchor of light. This is an anchor which allows fear to dissipate and allows humanity space to understand that the existence of fear does not mean that demise is imminent.

Instead, fear can be a gift – an indication of a path forward. A gift of understanding. A gift of learning.

Remember:

Growth comes in the light and in the dark, and in the known and in the unknown.

Personal Exploration Questions from Labradorite:

Use these questions for journaling, contemplation, or meditation; open your Akashic Records or the Akashic Records of Labradorite and ask:

1. How can I understand fear as a gift?
2. When do I fear the light of connection?
3. How can I expand my sense of connection within myself and with others?
4. What is the energy of Labradorite for me?

15

MALACHITE
CLEAR STREAMS

A copper carbonate mineral of a deep-green color.

Malachite led me to making my own jewelry. In my 20s, my eye surgeon father went to Africa to work in a small local clinics. One day a patient came asking to pay him in kind, displaying his wares. Dad accepted one strand in payment and insisted on paying for more. One strand he gave to me: a necklace of large malachite beads on thick black cotton thread already beginning to fray. I learned to restring the necklace and add a clasp. There is a heft and depth to the stones which feels very comforting to me. Sometimes, instead of wearing them, to absorb their support, I lay them beside me as I write.

. . .

Welcome! The energy of Malachite is about trickster energy and the energy of intelligence needed to reveal the absurdities in a situation.

Malachite helps uncover misstatements and mistruths – especially those used to incite fear.

Malachite comes into existence through the combination of pressure with what appears as opposing forces.

In the heart of Malachite is the balance between what appears to be oppositional in nature.

Thus, Malachite is very good at supporting motion toward truth without the fear of being exposed and being maligned simply because your opinion, your emotion, your thoughts, or your actions run counter to the majority voice within your environment.

Malachite is one of the main supporters of physical-spiritual integration. We support the ability to look at what's in opposition to whatever the deeper understanding may be. We see opposition as a new way of looking, a new way of approaching, or a new way of understanding.

This is an opportunity to move away from repetition towards new understanding, new integration, and new ways of dealing with the unexpected and the uncertainty of life.

Malachite is one of the older gemstones on the planet. Malachite appeared in the second manifestation of Earth at a time when the tectonic plates of earth were much more fluid but yet much more pressurized.

Malachite understands pressure – understands how to evolve within pressure – within being misunderstood or feeling exposed.

Malachite's point of spiritual balance comes in that ability to stand at the balance point between what seems to be two oppositional forces without judgment.

Malachite can transcend the situation and see how the integration of each brings the ability to see and understand life from a new and more empowered point of view.

Malachite's message to humanity:

Personal Power-Within emerges from the pressure to negate self.

When someone is able to deal with pressure and maintain a sense of self, they have fully ignited and claimed their power within. Malachite's basic energetic support to humanity opens the door to seeing undue pressure as the chance to take in deeper levels of awareness.

The pressure isn't to let go of what is important. The pressure is a motion to receive what is important in the moment regardless of the pressure.

Remember:

Personal Power-Within emerges from the pressure to negate self.

Personal Exploration Questions from Malachite:

Use these questions for journaling, contemplation, or meditation; open your Akashic Records or the Akashic Records of Malachite and ask:

1. How can I find balance between fun and seriousness in my life? In my work?
2. How can I deal with pressure through grace and ease?
3. What steps can I take to claim the depth of my personal power within?
4. What is the energy of Malachite for me?

16

MOLDAVITE
STAR POWER

Tektites or small, roundish, glassy stones, similar to Obsidian, strewn in the fields of Bohemia and Moravia. A borrowing of Moldau *from the German word for the Czech Republic river, the* Vltava.

I have had a tiny piece of Moldavite sitting on the small altar of my desk for many years. I pick it up and feel an Otherness which feels at peace and in balance. Moldavite feels almost plastic, like it's a creation of imagination. Its presence brings me solace and connection with all that exists beyond.

We come before you with hope in our hearts! Our energy is a combination of terrestrial and non-terrestrial energy.

While each gemstone has spiritual components, we, Moldavite, are made of forces and materials beyond the Earth plane. We are remnant pieces of huge asteroids and comets containing trace materials from the origins of stars and planets beyond your galaxy and your physical dimension.

We hold the seeds of stars and the death memories of universes long pass within your perspective of linear Earth time.

We hold the hopes and dreams of beings who have perished and who have yet to be born.

We represent the possibility of shifted vision and open understanding of potential beyond the limits of linear perspective.

We also represent the joy of exploration, of seeking beyond, traveling into the dark and into the light. Dark is but the unknown and yet to be understood.

Moldavite holds promise of what can be attained when the unknown is not feared and connection with all is embraced.

Our soul is the amalgamation of experience across seemingly opposing forces.

We have learned to transcend limitation through expanded understanding, never confusing not-knowing with can't-knowing. All can be known and understood eventually.

Only fear will convince that not-knowing is insurmountable.

In this moment, not-knowing may appear to be eternal and unfathomable. But this is purely a deceit born from limited awareness and the manipulation of fear.

Only within the deceit of fear can not-knowing be maintained as real. Through the metamorphosis of our "otherness" and with the heat and chill of intergalactic journey, Moldavite exhibits the possibility to transcend limitation and express truth within a newly perceived environment.

We hope that our amalgamation of physical and spiritual with this world and other-world demonstrates the capacity of humanity to transcend the antiquated manipulation of fear.

Our message for humanity:

Being different, move beyond the limits of fear on to your path for tomorrow.

Moving beyond fear allows for a fluidity – an opportunity to shift perspective within the energy of the moment.

Spiritual balance within the already-arrived physical-spiritual integration comes within awareness of shift, awareness of movement within the linear and the nonlinear.

Moldavite supports learning this shift and learning to find comfort both within the static and the dynamic.

This is a present moment awareness of experience. This is learning connection, both local and non-local, both physical and spiritual.

Balance for humanity is inherent between physical and spiritual, within the new energy and new Earth agreements for humanity.

In alignment with these agreements, we recommend the energy of power within to live life inside-out. Your power-within helps navigate an inner sense of being different as a positive opportunity.

When there is inner turmoil born of fear and domination, the temptation is to fall, or to disappear to maintain a sense of safety, however limited.

Held firmly, power within can perceive fear as manipulation. Power within can see that fear attempts to demean and belittle, to attack the Other, and to frighten rather than let the divine potential of self shine.

To recognize Other is to see divine possibility and the infinite and eternal nature of all creation.

We, Moldavite, come from Other not as warning but as greetings of potential and possibility of the amazing expressions you are and will absolutely become.

Begin within self to feel your divine essence and your eternal connection to All That Is.

Remember:

Being different, move beyond the limits of fear on to your path for tomorrow.

Personal Exploration Questions from Moldavite:

Use these questions for journaling, contemplation, or meditation; open your Akashic Records or the Akashic Records of Moldavite and ask:

1. How can I see whatever is different about me is an opportunity I have overlooked?
2. How can I respond to challenge without fear?
3. What can I do today to expand my path tomorrow?
4. What is the energy of Moldavite for me?

17

MORGANITE
ANGELIC PEACE

A pink translucent variety of beryl containing caesium.

When I was sixteen, my parents gave me a ring with a beautiful star ruby. When my daughter turned sixteen, I wanted to do the same for her. This is how I learned of the beauty of Morganite because my daughter's name is Morgaine. The stone has a beautiful clarity and true light pink hue I liked immediately and felt she would, too. And she does. For us both, a gift of peace.

We welcome you to our awareness – for this is our purpose on earth: Awareness.

We are of the ease of awareness. Not the push or the struggle. Rather that which comes easily when we quit the fight. When we stop pushing to do better, to do more, to be perfect.

We think this is much easier to describe than for you to do.

Trained to be highly productive, release seems contrary, the opposite of what is demanded.

How can anything be achieved without effort? You are taught to produce, to do, to achieve in order to gain whatever goal is set before you.

Yes, there are many times when effort is required. Doing nothing gets you nowhere.

However, the choice to pause is doing. Choice is always an active experience. Conscious choice is always engagement with life.

Choosing to let go of the struggle is an act of motion in life. Recognizing the need to pause is a sign of inner strength and a path to clarity – to the awareness which flows always transcendent to the struggle.

Energetically our soul, the soul of Morganite, intentionally attracts angelic energy to support this awareness. We do this because humanity interacts with the angelic energy as peaceful, calming, and protective.

We know the struggle to do comes from the push to protect and to stay safe.

The ability to pause and stand fully aware is difficult for humans.

However, with the current planetary shifts, we know humanity needs assistance in finding new ways of dealing with change.

Learning to shift from survive to thrive is aided by putting down the constant urge to fight.

Thrive has a chance when you learn to trust the ebb and flow, the active motion and the stillness of pause.

Within the stillness is the potential for seeing and understanding that which was hidden by activity.

The pause gives an opportunity to consider and to look from different angles.

The pause offers opportunity to question assumption and perceive the unexpected with less worry or concern.

Our energy holds for you the opportunity to learn about yourself away from outside opinion and influence.

Our energy gives you the option to shine light in the darker corners and see that life isn't quite as dire as activity might assume.

This pause offers the opportunity to see trouble at rest is different than trouble's pushiness.

With energy resting, you have the opportunity to reassess or reevaluate what you want and how you want to get there.

What may have felt impossible takes on a new perspective and brings forward new opportunity.

Our message for humanity:

Slow down. Pause.
Find your place of peace.
Now you are ready to proceed.

The pause is where you find trust and truth. Within the pause, hear what is obstructed by the clatter outside.

The pause is your path to peace.

You find this path only through the power of your personal choice to pause.

Your choice. Be in peace. Once again, remember:

Slow down. Pause.
Find your place of peace.
Now you are ready to proceed.

Personal Exploration Questions from Morganite:

Use these questions for journaling, contemplation, or meditation; open your Akashic Records or the Akashic Records of Morganite and ask:

1. What pushes at me to always be doing?
2. How can I be at peace with myself?
3. How can I learn to pause?
4. What is the soul message Morganite has for me today?

18

OBSIDIAN

ANGELIC TRANSITION

Volcanic glass formed from the rapid solidification of lava without crystallization.

For me Obsidian has been about absorption of that which prevents me from clear self-awareness and from unresisted shift and change. I use Obsidian to absorb what is no longer needed, as hurt and harm are released. Obsidian aids discovery and supports motion which has been stuck. Obsidian relieves me of pressure to be what I am not and supports me to be exactly who I am. Obsidian reminds me that I am in constant motion, a constant interaction of being and becoming. With Obsidian, I do not feel alone.

. . .

With one deep, singular voice, the Gemstone Guardians of Obsidian begin:

Let me tell you a story about fire and ice. For my soul is born within both, especially in the transition. My soul is embedded in transition, in the motion from one state to the seemingly opposite state. A transmutation of energy, of spirit to matter, of unknowable to knowing.

At first, I wanted to express only within fire. The heat which ignites activity. The spark, the dance, the joy to exist and share warmth. For fire is important to physical manifestation which I noticed within the motion of transition from one state of being to another. In this awareness, I claimed a new expression of fire into ice.

Ice contains the joy in its balanced, resonating state. Ice is energy transmuted from life. In this state of ice, I am about transition, the motion of release, of transferring existence from one state to another.

This energy – my energy – supports a fluidity which need not be named or contained. Rather supports release, supports the motion from one state of existence to another.

My soul has walked this path innumerable times because this is what brings me into being: the transition of soul transmutation.

I come into physical existence to support the physical need for transition and the release needed to follow this energetic path of life as physical-spiritual being.

I can do this because initially, I am fire, I am the heat of the soul dancing into being both spiritual and physical. Then I transition into ice with solid glass-like planes which smooth and reflect and which also absorb the energy which impedes release.

Release must precede transition. Release is letting go of the structure or framework of the departing state of existence. My fire state aids this release. A directed flame of release which judges not and instead sees the flames of possibility and the path toward the possibility. Not a foretelling for this is a limited linear perspective.

Rather, my seeing in this moment is of the infinite and eternal of this powerful spiritual-physical integration. With the release comes the transition, the motion forward not as separated flows, rather as an integrated whole. A holistic motion which arises from the synergy of *What Was* with *What Is* to create the expression of *What Will Be*. This is a transition of being to becoming to being. This is my creative intent: to support the external cycle of being-becoming, to being-becoming, to being-becoming.

This is the power which is ignited by the joining of seemingly opposites. Fire to ice, ice to fire – an eternal motion between opposites because of the willing choice to release structure and flow into essence.

This is where I find balance: in the transition. Like a scale finding balance between the polar opposites, between the up and down, the back and forth.

Balance in transition comes in the still point between up and down, in and out. It's the moment of release where neither label applies. This is the release point where the stillness needs no name, no definition. The transition happens naturally in the inherent pause of *What Is*.

Peace is found in the release. I watch as people push to maintain a non-beneficial state of existence, caught in labels of bad and good, right and wrong. They are stuck in yesterday, in *What Was* and is truly no longer.

This seems to be perpetuated by belief that self is unworthy, incapable of maintaining and living within true value and self-love.

Peace within body, mind, heart, and soul comes in the release of what no longer serves. Peace comes in the transition powered by release of *What Was* to move into the present moment of *What Is*, ready for the transition to *What Will Be*.

Judgment holds you in a stagnant pool of self-pity, and the tendency to blame others for life's events.

When this happens, hold me in your hand,. Allow my fire to burn away and release your burdens . In the lightness of release you transition into a new state of existence, supporting motion forward. The physical states of ice, water, and mist are now able to support further learning and understanding.

In this new state of existence, you're able to connect with new expression and new understanding. Your essence is now expressing your new flow of becoming. Being now open to experience the peace of your existence because you had the courage to release.

Let us speak about the motion of transition.

All energy is always in motion. For human beings, beyond physical body motion, energy's movement is seen and understood within the motion of self-awareness.

There are many directions possible in any moment. However, when self-awareness is ignored or denied, direction is chosen through habit. Most often, these are habits which no longer serve the person's deepest expression.

When self-awareness is weak, what is needed is courage to act without knowledge of the outcome. At first, this is very difficult to do without certainty or guarantee. Taking the step requires a beginning without knowing where the foot may rest in the motion. This is stepping into the unknown, into a darkness, into a fear.

This is the reason I assist transition. In the still point, *What Was* has already shifted form and *What Will Be* has not yet materialized. The still point can be interpreted as empty. We want to assure you that within transition, you are not alone. Quite the contrary, there are more there than you can imagine, more support and awareness which holds you precious, worthy of attention, worthy of love and support.

Loneliness appears because of uncertainty about the outcome. The inner sense of being the only one comes when the experience and awareness of transition is limited or feared.

The divine essence of you is maintained in any transition. What doesn't make it through is that which cannot transition because it no longer serves the best of you.

The power of self-awareness comes within the willingness to step forward and trust. Your willingness to trust the still point transition from one state of being into a new state of being.

My/Our message to you:

Self essence is empowered within both fire and ice.

There is no transition which can destroy you. The only trouble with transition comes in the resistance or the refusal.

Know you have the capacity for greatness by accepting the energetic motion of transition. Allow me into your life as reminder and companion in the moment to moment motions which make up your life. Empowered by transition, self-awareness becomes a path of joy, of discovery, and of self-appreciation.

As you journey, think of us and remember:

Self essence is empowered in the transition and in the
still point.
You are always both fire and ice.

P.S. Our pronouns (my, our) shift to reflect my constant state of transition.

Personal Exploration Questions from Obsidian:

Use these questions for journaling, contemplation, or meditation; open your Akashic Records or the Akashic Records of Obsidian and ask:

1. What is the nature of the fire essence of my self-awareness?
2. What is the nature of the ice essence of my self-awareness?
3. What is my experience at the still point of transition?
4. What is the truth of Obsidian for me?

19

ONYX
SOUL UNITY

A form of Chalcedony with plane layers of multiple colors.

Visiting my Grandmother Jessie was always so much fun when I was a little girl. She lived in a bright attic room in her sister's house and we got to sleep with her in her big four-post bed. My sister and I loved to ask her questions about all the things there, but especially her rings. When I was about 9 years old, she told us the story of her rings. The beautiful ruby ring came from her parents. The other ring came from the boy who asked her to marry him in high school. The ring was hexagonal with a beautiful gold scroll work and at the center of the hexagon was a diamond surrounded by Onyx. No this was not my mother's father, this was the boy her parents didn't want her to marry so they moved as she graduated from high school making her leave him behind. After my Grandmother passed, the engagement ring came to me as she had requested. And though I have now passed the ring to my daughter, my Grandmother is with me every day.

We began our journey in the fires and the heat of the earth and we also embrace the heat of the galaxy.

Over the millennia, humanity has associated the night sky with the unknown creating a limit to the incredible energy which surrounds the earth and moves into the geothermal expression of the planet.

We have embraced this heat as our own expression because at the deepest levels we are the energy of soul heat, soul light, soul reflection and the clarity is available within the minutia of linear existence.

As the Gemstone Guardians of Onyx, we are united. We are solid guardian expression and have no trouble being part of the depth of expression we represent.

Our mandate as Onyx is to support this depth in humanity and to help humanity see and experience depth as a positive force of change and a positive support for change.

We move slowly so you will not trip and miss what is authentic, aligned, and balanced within present moment expression and your steps towards the future of your human experience.

There is clarity and unity when one is not afraid. This is clarity of experience which we support and hope to empower within you.

Again, we will emphasize the importance that our energy is the foundation of our unity. Our energy of unity is a field of synthesis, of synchronicity, and of inherent integration.

Our message for humanity:

Unity does not erase the individual.

Embedded within the old energy leaving the planet, there is the belief that unity is only possible by eliminating any sense of the individual. The belief sees unity is only possible within the spiritually well-trained and well-educated. But when unity is achieved, the individual can lose self. This belief maintains that the unknown or the nonlocal is not friendly or is dangerous. The agenda of fear maintains this belief as a form of coercion. But in this day of planetary shift, this belief is false.

When you are clear about who you are, you are less worried about what you don't know. You deal with uncertainty in a very different way.

You're not about controlling. You're not about dominating. You're not about obliterating those of whom you are afraid.

Fear drives the sense of obliteration, the sense care needs to be taken or you will lose the important parts of who you are.

This is what fear and domination does, turning the stranger and the unknown into enemies to fear, to avoid, and to conquer as way of maintaining its own weird expression of individual obliteration.

Fear has no problem if the individual relinquishes power within and sinks into the mindless mass. Within what is controlled exists the status of power.

Those who do not submit are turned into the unknown stranger who must be opposed and obliterated.

Instead, connection drives experience to become engaged to see all people.

Remember:

Unity does not erase the individual.

Personal Exploration Questions from Onyx:

Use these questions for journaling, contemplation, or meditation; open your Akashic Records or the Akashic Records of Onyx and ask:

1. How is my fear of missing out driven by the belief of obliteration?
2. How do I cancel myself or others?
3. How can I move forward in my life within a sense of unity?
4. What is the energy of Onyx for me?

20

OPAL
HEART FIRE

A form of hydrated silica in color from white and orange to blue and black. Most valued forms with colorful iridescence. Earliest samples came from India. Latin opalus *connected to the older Sanskrit,* upala, *precious stone.*

I first learned of Opal from my Grammy Flora when I was seven years old and she explained the significance of Opal for the two of us. Both born in October, Opal is our birthstone. I felt a connection with my Grandmother because of how she taught me to love life and to enjoy the fruits of our love and labor. I can't look at an Opal without thinking of her and her unique spark within. She helped light my fire and I will always be thankful for her gift.

We welcome you to the land of Opal!

Opal is an energy of collective awareness and experience.

We are also of fire light – an active energy of awareness and experience similar to starlight. Within Physical Reality, our light begins as a photon across the wave continuum. We are a dance with the element of fire and of love.

Our soul story is one of coming together within the connection of All That Is. We are a fused energy of many souls who are drawn to the combined experience of love and joy, within the experience of manifested existence.

Within the arena of Earth, we are here to support the joy of exchange and connection.

In a world where fear perpetuates fear, we are here to challenge this assumption and to foster the connection inherent within all manifestation as we enjoy our intrinsic connection one with the other.

We are also of the energy of harmony and of balance – a balance where the awareness of resonance guides dissimilar to find balance where the intrinsic nature of each is maintained. Rather than a leveling which attempts to homogenize reducing fire to a muddled experience.

Fire is what manifests individual experience. This may seem at odds with our collective awareness – but we are not joined to make all energy similar. We are joined to support individual difference, individual *fire*.

This is a very important differentiation. We as Opal lift awareness of individual fire, of personal story. *Fire* gives birth to *Word* and the capacity to be clear about and express personal story which emerges from personal fire.

Personal power within is an expression of fire – the creative soul story fire. As Opal, we are here to support this personal emergence and to hold the sacred space which gives support to connection, harmony, and balance.

As an integrated whole, Opal loves to hold space for all integrated experience because our energetic fire reflects the light of spiritual-physical integration for all humanity.

Because of our focus on balance and harmony, our energy supports awareness within of where balance aligns and is challenged.

Plus our support is the energy of acceptance of depth and of personal power spark. This spark is the transmutational shift of all creative energy. This spark exists within each individual. This spark is the origin of all creative action. This spark is the origin of breath.

Fire exists because of this spark. The spark is a transformative energy which transmutes energy into *Fire* expression. A motion of *Air* supports the spark as energy moves from potential to form containing potential.

For those struggling with integration, we inhibit judgment which will stand in the way of integration because of fear. For integration demands the release of control, the release of destructive criticism, and the acceptance of personal power.

Power in one aspect is *Fire*, an experience of potential to form as a continuous experience of soul awareness.

Spiritual balance is within the integration of being and becoming. As Earth progresses, integration of physical and spiritual will deepen and provide a canvas of balance for further exploration and creative effort. We as Opal are here to support this growth.

Our message for humanity:

Love is the fire of free personal expression.

Through connection with All That Is comes the awareness of the depth of personal expression. When the individual believes in self, believes in self as worthy, then personal power becomes a spark of love – a spark which births Fire as the flame of uninhibited power within, unrestrained, free to flow and express, free to see the magic of all flows, excited to connect and experience personal flow and personal interaction with all flow.

Love is this experience and this expression because of this experience. For the spark is love. Love is the transmutative experience of Fire. Love is Fire.

We believe we are here to help humanity move beyond fear by embracing the creative capacity and support of personal power which emerges in recognition of infinite and eternal connection.

The answer to fear is not to separate and divide. Instead the more beneficial motion is to recognize the loving support of connection. Within connection, personal power within and creative expression expands and expresses inherent *Fire* and Love.

Let this settle into your awareness!

Remember:

Love is the fire of free personal expression.

Personal Exploration Questions from Opal:

Use these questions for journaling, contemplation, or meditation; open your Akashic Records or the Akashic Records of Opal and ask:

1. What destroys the fire of my heart?
2. How can I enjoy my heart's spark?
3. How does my fire fuel my capacity to love?
4. What is the energy of Opal for me?

21

PETRIFIED WOOD
ESSENTIAL ALCHEMY

Wood turned to mineral or stone through the process of petrification.

I have always been fascinated with the idea of wood turned to stone. As a child, I heard of the Petrified Forrest and wanted to see – wanted to know how it was possible to have wood turn to stone. This is alchemy in nature demonstrating the possibilities of transmutation – demonstrating a process without which can happen within. No wonder I was intrigued – and still am.

Energetically, we are the alchemy of transmutation. We exemplify the transformation of essence at the primary structural level where DNA retains its coherency while cellular structure is fundamentally changed through sustained physical pressure.

This is an obvious metaphor for life, where intense pressure yields a new and unexpected form.

We want to share pressure with you so you might experience the alchemy of your soul within your physical life on Earth. For as you say, with the pressure of transmutation, you may live the same life, but life will never be the same.

The pressure of change can be transmutative – meaning the essence of being can shift beyond imagination into a beautiful new expression.

Take our physical shift as example, where the concerted pressure over time moves the porous cell into solid, impervious structure. The pressure creates strength in a new direction. Though, as with all physical substance, is still capable and liable to disintegration. Dust to dust.

However, the interim experience turns attention from one form towards the unanticipated possibilities of another form. Life transformed can be life transmuted. The shift in essence restructures the framework of life. What once absorbed water, now repels. What once swayed in the wind can now resist movement and yet becomes susceptible to erosion.

This means change has unexpected consequences as well as unimagined possibility.

Our message for humanity:

Allow the pressure of life to refine your essence within the miraculous and the divine.

If you turn your attention to only what you know and what you expect, your life dries and becomes shallow, arid, narrowed.

If, instead, you turn your attention to your experience and awareness in this moment and allow the unknown and unexpected to reveal essence in this moment, the flow of your life yields opportunity to experience expanded essence.

Whether you turn your back on opportunity or you turn to face the sun of today and tomorrow, there is always pressure. In one direction, the pressure is to deny self, to denigrate personal choice, and undermine personal power. In another direction, pressure freezes intention and instills fear, making any motion in life near impossible. In yet another direction, pressure becomes the crucible for change, for embracing release of pain and sorrow, for making personal choice despite fear.

The stone of wood is the energy of clear personal choice in the face of pressure and the presence of fear.

Squeezed to the brink of what can no longer be endured, the closed door no longer matters. A new door now beckons. What was perceived as breakdown transmutes through pressure into breakthrough.

Transformed. Transmuted. Life is and will be forever changed.

That you are essential is always true even though your essence has expanded beyond imagination.

Remember:

Allow the pressure of life to refine your essence within the miraculous and the divine.

Personal Exploration Questions from Petrified Wood:

Use these questions for journaling, contemplation, or meditation; open your Akashic Records or the Akashic Records of Petrified Wood and ask:

1. What one belief can I shift or release in this moment which will transmute the essence of my life?
2. How do I underestimate myself?
3. How can I create miracles?
4. What message does Petrified Wood have for me today?

22

RHODONITE
NEW BALANCE

A manganese-containing mineral with rose-pink or brownish tabular crystals.

Learning of Rhodonite has helped me to see that there are always new beginnings within our planet and within our lives. The earth shifts and changes and brings forth new motions as needed. We, too, shift and change and sometimes are able to allow new motion to be part of our experience. Rhodonite reflects this eternal cycle of learning and growing. An essence of both what was and what will be.

W e welcome you into our energy. We want to share with you our story so that you can become familiar and comfortable with our energy.

Compared to other Gemstone Guardians, we act both in union and individually. We are connected energy with solitary representation. In this way, we are much like humans.

Our energy arose strictly on Earth within the geological forces of approximately 500,000 years ago. Our initial motion into form was guided by Quartz in response to the need for support for the coming age of human development and intelligence. The Earth Council, understanding the intention and possibilities of humanity and, at that time, undertaking the development of the Human-Earth Agreements, were involved in forming much that would support humanity in the many centuries to come.

Essentially, Rhodonite answered the Call to provide physical support to the spiritual nature of humanity. We are integrated much in the same way where who we are physically is intentionally integrated with a deep and profound spiritual awareness.

Because of this inherent alignment with the deepest of human nature, our energy is uniquely designed to support the current human re-alignment with their spiritual-physical natures.

In the sense, Rhodonite holds the energy presence and awareness of re-alignment. We are about the return to balance, about a reminder that balance, harmony, and alignment exist always, are of present moment existence. Not to be created but remembered and claimed.

Our message for humanity:

On deep breath-in is the memory of alignment with divine transcendence.

On deep breath-out is the return within to balance with All That Is.

We are here to remind you that you can live within the incredible alignment of who you are physically and who you are spiritually.

For several thousand years, the external message has been that human beings are corrupted and unworthy of divine balance. While this provided an interesting path to develop the mind and body, this was a message that was inherently untrue.

At the heart of every human being is the capacity to engage fully within the alignment of physical nature with spiritual nature. This is an alignment of body, mind, heart, and soul.

To achieve this balance and integration is simply to put down the externalized judgment on humanity and claim the truth of you as worthy and capable of divine alignment while being physically present on Earth.

Earth is your chosen home for your current incarnation. Thus, it is both possible and encouraged for you to claim your divine birthright as the magnificent being you are and can always become.

By living within this promise, you no longer have the need for fear to dominate or denigrate others. Dominion over Earth by a scared, controlling populace can be replaced by the inherent harmony and connection experienced by all creation on Earth.

The place to begin is within you. Release self-judgment and self-condemnation. Release disbelief and mistrust. Release blame and shame.

You begin with one breath. On inhale, feel the tiny motion within you which remembers self-alignment – a motion which does not resist, ignore, or deny.

As you release and exhale, feel balance within you connect with the balance around you. Again, this may be incredibly faint.

However, as you begin this process, what you will bump up against is the belief and habit of humanity's unworthiness and the fear to believe anything else. Like a film or shadow blocking the light, slowly the misunderstanding can be peeled away in small steps and gentle moments.

Your re-alignment with your spiritual-physical integrated self will happen over time. This will require patience as you allow the tiny bits and the overwhelmingly huge beliefs to drop away. There will be those who want to convince you of your folly at attempting the impossible.

But we, Rhodonite, are present now to remind you of the true nature of your body and soul united here, now on Earth.

We are present to help you remember, to help you re-claim the very best of you in balance with All That Is.

Remember:

On deep breath-in is the memory of alignment with divine transcendence.

On deep breath-out is the return within to balance with All That Is.

Personal Exploration Questions from Rhodonite:

Use these questions for journaling, contemplation, or meditation; open your Akashic Records or the Akashic Records of Rhodonite and ask:

1. Why is my soul present in a human body on Earth at this time?
2. What stands in the way of me remembering my alignment and balance with All That Is?
3. How can I live in spiritual-physical integration within a world which wants to dominate and ignore my truth?
4. What message of truth does Rhodonite have for me today?

23

ROSE QUARTZ
HEART CRYSTAL

A translucent pink variety of quartz

Rose Quartz has always been a presence on the edge of my life. A presence that I acknowledged but didn't feel the need to bring closer. Not because I didn't want or need Rose Quartz. Rather this was its place while other stones gathered nearer. As Heart Crystal, I feel a deep affinity with my futuristic nature and an excitement of possibility to come and dreams which will unfold in time.

First, let us say Rose Quartz is a false reference for this gemstone formation. Please address us properly as

Heart Crystal Quartz. We thank you for your respect and attention.

We are a gemstone which has had a very active presence in the world, and we feel this new name is a better representative of our energetic intent.

We are a gemstone energy which has shifted our energy over the last hundred years or so partly in response to Earth shifts but also to support and embrace the shifts of humanity.

While we have always been responsive to the issues of the heart and self-love, our shift is to support the heart shift during this motion into spiritual-physical integration.

There is a crystalline structure developing within the human heart which is coming forth to support the heart development needed for this integration. There are other Gemstone Guardians involved in this new, emerging, creative energy.

Let us first speak of the crystalline structure. This is not a rigid structure, and it is not fixed in intention, other than to support the heart's motion within this new energy on the planet. In this energy, both heart and soul are coming together in a reciprocating personal interaction and integration which harmonizes the energies to work together rather than the more combative energies of the past.

Even we as Gemstone Guardians are learning this positive, collective approach though some Guardians are holding an anchor point for the past to be the past.

As Heart Crystal, the primary effort and support of our energy is to create an anchored flow point for the human heart to feel capable to address fear straight on instead of a flight from that which threatens (or seems to). In the energy of the past 3000 years, all gemstones had different overall intention within the Earth energy and with humanity.

Thus, the crystalline structure is a matrix for restructuring the fear response. This is a development happening slowly on the planet.

We first came forward in one of Earth's first physical expressions. In this early expression, Earth was just learning the intricacies of humanity's potential integration of body, mind, heart, and soul.

This is a complex expression which took several Earth forms until the current one emerged in Earth's previous incarnation..

Then and now, our collective intention as both Rose Quartz and Heart Crystal Quartz is to support the deepest and clearest human heart expression possible by the human being.

The human heart is a unique expression within the history of Earth for it is capable of empathy, of vulnerability, of compassion, and of the deepest love.

Love emerges first as the full attention of All That Is for the newly emerging soul. This attention is our first mandate: We see you. We acknowledge your energetic intention to express your deepest love for yourself and for others.

Our second mandate: Fear is a choice and need not be an obstacle.

Our third mandate: Love is the clearest path to express the depth of integration of body, mind, heart, and soul.

Our message for humanity

Your deepest capacity supports expression and connection without resistance to the unknown, without hesitation, without fear, without hate.

To equate the unknown with that which should be avoided, ignored, or diminished creates false boundaries and negativity.

With the new crystalline structures emerging and within the physical-spiritual aspects of your heart, you now have direct access to conscious choice of how you respond to and live with fear.

This structure provides additional support to feel connected and not alone against the wiles of life. Connection can exist beyond hesitation and hatred.

Instead, the shift is to feel and live within this sense of connection so that fear becomes the focus of choice rather than an energy which overwhelms and limits the sense of personal capacity.

Along with other Guardians, we as Heart Crystal Quartz are here to support the emergence of deepest heart capacity within the newest expressions of body, mind, heart, and soul integration.

Remember:

Your deepest capacity supports expression and connection without resistance to the unknown, without hesitation, without fear, without hate.

Personal Exploration Questions from Heart Crystal/Rose Quartz:

Use these questions for journaling, contemplation, or meditation; open your Akashic Records or the Akashic Records of Heart Crystal/ Rose Quartz and ask:

1. In my life, what is love? What is fear?
2. In my life, how can I better deal with the unknown?
3. How is the emerging crystalline structure supporting my physical-spiritual integration?
4. What is the energy of Heart Crystal Quartz for me?

24

RUBY

GENUINE BEAUTY

A valuable precious stone in color from deep crimson or purple to light red. A borrowing from the Old French rubi, *a precious red stone.*

Ruby calls to me through its inherent authenticity. Though not the kind which attempts to show itself based on falseness and distraction. While I see Ruby as the essence of beauty, Ruby is not beautiful just because of its color. Ruby's deep beauty comes from within, in balance with inherent capacity and heart-driven awareness of what is real and true and beautiful. Ruby reminds me that just as I am is the beauty I am afraid I do not possess nor will ever find. Ruby brings me back to my beautiful self.

. . .

Welcome to the energy of Ruby! Ruby has been a part of Earth emergence from the very, very beginning. Our red is about the balance and integration of our energies.

We began as an energy focused on grounding and balance. We are still of this energy, and we have also moved into energy related to the essence of beauty, the physical experience of beauty, and the clarity which emerges when one is connected to the beauty of any person, situation, or energetic expression.

We bring the energy of the earth up into a space of spectacular focus of beauty, awareness, and balance.

We are the energy of excited anticipation.

We are the energy of joy. We are the beauty of joy. In the awareness of joy comes the ability to find balance within the unknown.

Do not feel exposed when your beauty receives attention. In our motion into physical form, we bring forward the energy of depth and express this depth through the solidity of our form. We are also expressing the idea that there can be clarity. Know the ability to see balance reveals the clarity available in any moment.

If you stand in joy and if you stand with the clarity of excited anticipation, then you have the ability to see and eliminate whatever fear may be contained within the present moment.

We come forward within the creative intent of our physical manifestation. This reflects this sense of joy and excited anticipation of the unknown.

We are here to provide the sense of joy as a touchstone for those who are moving through the trials and tribulations of physical-spiritual integration.

This integration is not an easy path. This integration is troubling for those who want to only work with what is known and with what is 100% certain.

But we come to say that excited anticipation does not require certainty.

Life is about the adventure.

Life is about the journey into the unknown.

This is what our energy as Ruby is here to support.

Our point of spiritual balance comes within this joy to live life as explorer.

While clarity in this moment may help fuel motion forward, clarity should not create a barrier or a limit from future motion because of uncertainty,

We are here to help you deal with uncertainty.

Our message for humanity:

Uncertainty is a gift from the future.

To help you discern your next step forward if you demand that fear, ambiguity, and the unknown be conquered and destroyed before you can live your life – you will live your life in the smallness of your limited vision and the weakness that will hinder your ability to find within your capacity for profound integration.

When you can claim a life for yourself, where you are not distracted or intimidated by fear, you have the possibility to learn, to expand, and to move forward into a greater expression of who you are at the deepest levels body, mind, heart, and soul.

You may think you are not enough. We want you to know that this is not true. Let go that which is not supportive of you in your fullness and clarity.

You do not need to be fearful. Life is a process to overcome your own fear.

For there is great love for you and great awareness of your capacity.

Ask your questions and you can move forward into an expanded awareness of who you are and can become.

Stand in your beauty and trust yourself as more than enough to walk the waves of uncertainty.

You got this!

There is naught but love for you always from us and the transcendent.

Remember:

Uncertainty is a gift from the future.

Personal Exploration Questions from Ruby:

Use these questions for journaling, contemplation, or meditation; open your Akashic Records or the Akashic Records of Ruby and ask:

1. What makes me anxious about the future?
2. How can I live in peace with uncertainty?
3. What is the superpower of my beauty?
4. What is my relationship with the energy of Ruby?

25

SELENITE
LIQUID LIGHT

A gypsum in a crystalline form. From the Latin meaning moonstone.

Did you know Selenite dissolves in water? I didn't until I tried purifying a piece the way I do with most of my gemstones: salt, water, and moonlight. At first, I thought someone had taken the piece – but that didn't make sense because I lived in the country at the time. I called the store where I purchased the Selenite wand. The store owner laughed and said she needed to make the sign larger. What sign, I asked. The one which says Selenite dissolves in water. Oh. Good to know. I've been careful ever since. Plus, I've realized Selenite has its own purifying system — it seems to really like sage.

. . .

We, the Gemstone Guardians of Selenite, want to take another path with you.

Like Quartz, we are part of the original formative energy of gemstones, of Earth, and of other physical planetoid environments.

Like Moldavite, we are both Earth and other than Earth. Like Quartz we have a crystalline structure. We also have a fluid connection with the cell structure of water.

Humanity has -- or at least can experience -- the same crystalline, fluid, *Other* expression. Within all humans is the capacity to be one with the fluid expression of physical life.

But it is the assumptions of an outdated way of thinking and perceiving which keeps most from releasing the false limitation and learning to experience the boundless fluidity which is within the foundation of humanity.

We are here to help humanity perceive and feel this fluidity. We are here to demonstrate connection across perceived differences.

Differences don't actually create separation. Separation occurs in the *belief* that difference is synonymous with separation.

Within fluidity, difference is discernment of where and how connection exists.

If you think you are different, do you feel separated? If so, what you are feeling is a discernment much like understanding red is not blue. However, each color is its own perception of light refraction.

Even to prefer red to blue is not inherently judgment -- rather a similar awareness of inner difference or preference.

The awareness is not rejection. Awareness is discernment.

Our message for humanity:

To discern difference is not judgment and difference is not separation.

All is connected, valued, and unique.

Judgment is at the heart of physical-spiritual separation. Judgment is the belief there is only one right way to perceive anything.

Judgment is born of fear, of the unknown, and the unpredictable. Judgment -- or the attempt to move away from its control -- wants to say that the problem is difference. We say the issue rests with thinking difference cannot be noticed or identified.

This is a false narrative which forgets that each soul is a unique expression of All That Is. Difference is inherent, intrinsic.

When we forget what brings us here -- the choice to experience our unique soul expressions -- the door for fear, manipulation, shame, denial, and annihilation opens and leaks repressive energy geared to making us forget the true nature of self, body, mind, heart, and soul.

Your true nature is boundless. YOU -- all of you -- is a uniquely powerful expression of divine energy which has unlimited capacity.

Simply put, you're here now to uncover and remember this boundless unlimited nature. Discernment of difference is simply awareness of your unique expression. Just as every piece of Selenite is not exactly the same, the same is true for humanity.

As said many times before, there is more commonality than difference.

The difference reflects you learning to know yourself.

To Know Thyself requires awareness of that which is not-thyself. Differentiation is creation, an energetic flow of love begetting life.

Celebrate your awareness and release fear of difference. Life will explode bringing expansion beyond imagination. Love self and other for your difference and life becomes safe and the unlimited becomes your possibility.

Remember:

To discern difference is not judgment and difference is not separation.

All is connected, valued, and unique.

Personal Exploration Questions from Selenite:

Use these questions for journaling, contemplation, or meditation; open your Akashic Records or the Akashic Records of Selenite and ask:

1. How am I fluid like Selenite?
2. Why am I afraid or concerned about being different?
3. How does All That Is value me? How can I value myself?
4. What is the energy of Selenite for me?

26

SODALITE
LIMINAL STARLIGHT

A sometimes transparent, greenish blue stone occurring in some igneous stone, containing aluminum, silica, and sodium.

Sodalite is a beautiful stone which always appears to me as one of deep experience. There is a collective awareness which inspires me to look beyond what I think I know. To consider that I don't know everything. To ponder the edges. To let go. To fly.

We welcome you to our energetic awareness. Our energy story is one of amalgamation of heart and body, and light within the unknown.

Within the Earth plane, our energy is about what is known and what can be known. We stand at the threshold, guide to the journey of self-discovery. We are master energy of What Is and What Can Be.

Our energy comes from across the infinite galactic expression of starlight in all its infinite forms and expressions. We are energy which has many non-terrestrial forms made manifest on Earth in her current incarnation.

We are very much of the present moment and assist humanity to be present to the truth of What Is in this moment.

We also assist with releasing blocks and obstacles to clarity and truth. We support a calm, even-handed assessment of the roots of denial and deception. For energetically, we are a firm foundation for clear awareness and truth in the moment.

Our message to humanity:

Truth is only painful when its emerging presence breaks down deceit, denial, and ignorance.

Take a deep breath and allow the broken bits to fly away.

The light of awareness breaks down the foundations of lies and mistruths. Overwhelm comes when the balance of clarity hasn't yet shifted equilibrium past the pain of deceit. Instead of relying on old habits and expectation of perfect or right action, take a deep breath and allow balance to appear within you. Balance is not made or created. Balance is received, appearing beyond assumption and expectation.

Balance and personal truth do not require giant steps or right action. These create resistance and obstacle. Instead, allow breath in to restore inner awareness and allow the gentle arrival of the presence of balance. A soft light. A gentle approach.

Sodalite energetically supports gentle inner acceptance of self. A self which is inherently capable of deep expression. A self divinely connected always. A self which is by design of the terrestrial and the non-terrestrial. For come are the days in which humanity is re-learning and re-acknowledging our divine connection, and infinite and eternal expression.

Light within expresses as divine light. Connection within expresses as the transcendent nature of body, mind, heart, and soul. Truth shines in this light and eliminates the self-imposed barriers.

We are emissaries of light, and we say to you:

As a phoenix, within soul's light you can arise from the ashes and claim your truth.

Deep breath!

Now: Stand and Shine!

Remember:

Truth is only painful when its emerging presence breaks down deceit, denial, and ignorance.

Take a deep breath and allow the broken bits to fly away.

Personal Exploration Questions from Sodalite:

Use these questions for journaling, contemplation, or meditation; open your Akashic Records or the Akashic Records of Sodalite and ask:

1. What do I release so I may stand and shine?
2. What patterns of denial do I habitually turn to when I feel challenged or overwhelmed?
3. How do I hold myself back from asking for what I want?
4. What messages does Sodalite have for me today?

27

SUGILITE
TRANSCENDENT CONNECTION

A relatively rare pink to purple cyclosilicate mineral first noted by Japanese scientist, Kenichiro Sugi, in 1944. Other notable sources include Canada and South Africa. Sugalite or Sugilite is literally the stone of Sugi.

Sometimes I meet a person or I experience an event which strikes me with a profound depth, realizing all of sudden: I am looking into the depths of the universe. I am connecting with the transcendence beyond me. I am one of many points of connection within the infinite and eternal. This was my first experience of Sugilite. A depth. A boundlessness. Unexpected. I was in a store, looking at a collection of stones. Sugilite caught my attention not because it jumped out and waved its hands. No, there was no attempt. That's what caught my attention. I picked up the piece before me and felt overwhelmed by the gravity of the stone. Then within me I felt a shift, a motion within me which brought me to resonance with the depth of the stone. That's how Sugilite came into my life.

———————————

I 'm one of the newer Gemstone Guardians.

Though my energy has been part of Earth for many thousands of year, I have only recently risen to the surface.

Now is the time for my emergence. Now is the time for the energy I support to come forward.

What I bring together energetically is a motion to integrate not just physical and spiritual but to also integrate the ancient energies with the emerging energies. I bring together what was known with what is unknown.

I speak of an emergence and an integration of past with future, that the present perceives the direction to find balance and harmony.

Energetically, the basis of my energy is about resonance and alignment.

My energy is especially resonance and alignment with that which is freshly emerging as possibility within the planet and within the experience of humanity.

I raise the ability to understand that life is not about superficial or shallow.

Understanding of balance certainly. However, the deepest balance comes through the understanding of that which initially appears to be in conflict, but with further exploration comes much deeper perception.

This is a motion to allow the incomprehensible to become clear and present truth.

Part of the motion of physical-spiritual integration is to increase the tolerance for ambiguity. This is an energy to become mindful of how context can shift the appreciation for truth in the moment.

When looking at the past, it is possible to understand where truth was to become aware of how truth has shifted into this moment. This raises the awareness that truth will shift again as you move into the future.

However, remember correctly identifying truth in the past doesn't necessarily mean that prediction of truth in the future will be accurate.

What's most important is that the awareness of the motion from past to present helps you move forward. Not because of guarantee but because you are aware of the shifts and changes inherent within truth.

Thus, my energy is very much about supporting tolerance of the unknown especially as energy moves forward into the unknown of the future.

My point of spiritual balance comes in the peaceful coexistence of resonance and dissonance. Eliminating dissonance is not the point. Rather understand integration occurs within the balance of dissonance and resonance.

Within this balance is the motion from this moment to the future – whatever the future might hold.

On Earth, there is now a shift in polarity. This is a beginning of a new perception. As you grow and open, you will begin to understand more of this story because by definition, the future is of the unknown.

My message for humanity:

Learn to love ambiguity for in the unknown is the direction to your future.

When you avoid what is unknown and unexpected, you freeze yourself in this moment, with your face towards the past.

The only way to move forward into the future is bring yourself to the present so that you may face the future hopefully and with excitement and high anticipation.

When that's not possible, be aware of resistance pulling you down and away from the central nexus of your personal power: this present moment.

I must speak of power because the dynamics of power on Earth and for humanity are shifting and changing. What a hundred years ago would have remained quiet, in this moment cannot be silent. There are many who are in fear and can only choose to live their life in fear.

Together, all of the Gemstone Guardians have this wish for humanity: fear need not be a choice. As Guardians, our mission, our mandate is to help humanity through this period of shift and change into a place of balance.

Not that problems go away.

However, the method to resolve trouble is to move away from blame and judgment into honest assessment of what works and what does not work.

We want dearly for you to hear what we are trying to express! This is a book not just about the Gemstone Guardians, but of global shift and how to live at peace with yourself within this kind of shift.

Within this global shift is a motion of responsibility.

A motion of clarity.

A motion of releasing judgment.

If there is anything that we could have humanity hear is that we are of the All.

This means that each person has their own perspective of truth. Empowerment is not about making others believe as you.

Empowerment is seeking to understand these perspectives that are held within the hearts of every being on the planet, within every motion of energy including people, animals, plants – everything!

Harmony with nature demonstrates how there can be harmony for All.

Remember:

**Learn to love ambiguity for in the unknown is the
direction to your future.**

Personal Exploration Questions from Sugilite:

Use these questions for journaling, contemplation, or meditation; open your Akashic Records or the Akashic Records of Sugilite and ask:

1. What keeps me from connecting with the depth of my heart?
2. How can I make peace with ambiguity and the unknown?
3. What will assist me to be fully present in my life?
4. What is the energy of Sugilite for me?

28

TOURMALINE
SOUL SPARK

A brittle pyro-electric mineral, occurring in crystals, which is massive, compact, and columnar, originally obtained from Sri Lanka. The spelling follows the French form.

Tourmaline holds a quiet spot in my life. A quiet sentinel holding space for me to find myself and stay present when the going gets tough. Life is not for either of us about flashy appearances. Rather a quiet Witness of all which is possible. A quiet peace. A quiet awareness of self.

W elcome! We want to introduce ourselves. We are the Guardians of Tourmaline and we want to tell you our story.

We are a group energy which provides protection at the edges and boundaries.

This may seem broad but within all learning is the edge of the unknown and unexpected. These edges are mandatory for personal growth. These edges help differentiation and assist with shift and change. Sometimes edges are felt like tumultuous cliffs. Sometimes edges are fluid, soft, easier to transverse, though both hold deep, unseen pockets and trenches, which can divert attention and challenge ease.

We, Tourmaline, provide the necessary attention needed so that one does not feel alone on the journey. We are not here to eliminate edges, instead our energetic support provides a sense or awareness that the seemingly solitary is not alone or without support.

We are, however, very clear that we will not **do** for anyone. Each person is responsible for their own journey, for their own desire to be guide for the journey of experience.

The journey of the soul is infinite and eternal in nature. While each soul is guided by individual intent, the soul is also part of the ebb and flow of the infinite and the eternal, and thus aware of the soul's potential to express and experience existence within the infinite and eternal.

The first experience of edges comes in how each soul flow is similar yet different, one from the other.

Within physical form, this awareness of differentiation can sharpen edges and deflect motion. The physical being can have both reactions and responses to this awareness.

Reaction emerges within fear or avoidance.

Response is a choice to engage or learn.

As Guardians of the edges, our energy supports response and the motion away from reaction. From fear to acceptance of *What Is*.

Thoughtless reaction creates an inner sense that edges must be avoided. Within response, edges and boundaries can behave as guidance and the sources of protection that they are.

Protection in this sense is not about defending safety. Here, protection is the energetic support necessary to feel comfortable or open to the unknown and the unexpected. This is the energetic stance necessary to begin and deepen physical-spiritual integration.

Our energy is of prime importance now and over the next ten years, especially for those looking to deepen their integration of body, mind, heart, and soul.

Tourmaline helps soften and understand edges, allowing body and mind to interact and learn from heart and soul.

Plus, the interaction is a feedback loop. Body and mind show heart and soul how to interact and be at peace with the boundaries of physical existence.

Heart and soul introduce body and mind to the delights of the unknown and the connections of spirit within all.

Our message for humanity:

All is possible.

The outdated reaction to edges is to think limitation, impossible, incapable. Yet within the awareness of physical-spiritual integration, edges are the possibilities of the unknown.

Thus, the issue is not one of incapacity. Instead, this is an issue of navigation – of how you learn to move through whatever approaches.

Instead of asking whether you are capable of keeping yourself safe, learn a new perspective.

Within integration, the soul introduces and guides body, heart, and mind to the intrinsic sense of worth and capacity inherent within all human beings.

Within this perspective comes the awareness that ALL is possible.

Thus the primary question for your journey is this:

In this moment, *HOW* is all possible?

In this moment at the edge of my soul's infinite and eternal possibility, what is my next step? Asking this question provides a framework to support your life, your spiritual practice, and your life's journey. There are no right or wrong answers. Simply, a way to stay clear of the knee-jerk reaction of habit and fear.

We also will speak of personal power within. For this inner personal awareness of the possibilities of power within can only come forth when there is awareness of edges. The edge helps distinguish between I Am and I Am Not. There is nothing to grow, develop, and expand if one is not aware of self.

This is an important point to make because awareness of self is the beginning of all personal and spiritual growth. Without self-awareness there is no way to access personal capacity, the beginning edges of personal growth, or claim personal power.

Possibility begins with the awareness of possibility.

The soul begins in the differentiation of I Am and I Am Not. Personal growth and meaningful awareness begin in the self's ability to discern I Am. In the discernment comes the awareness of self. In the discernment comes the identification of personal boundaries. In the discernment comes the ability to see and exercise personal choice and self-determination.

Without this sense of I Am and the emergence of self-awareness, possibility is not present as seeable or understandable.

We write of this because when possibility seems bleak or absent, find the threads of possibility by looking for self. Look for your deepest sense of I Am. For within the connection of I Am is the connection to all possibility.

This is a present moment awareness and one in which you must be fully present to *What Is*.

Layer by layer is an unfolding of self within the possibility you both allow and accept without denial or rejection.

To reach and live within the deepest perspectives of your personal power within, begin by opening to I AM and *What Is*. Trust yourself to choose your path.

Remember:

All is possible.

Personal Exploration Questions from Tourmaline:

Use these questions for journaling, contemplation, or meditation; open your Akashic Records or the Akashic Records of Tourmaline and ask:

1. How do I understand who I Am?
2. How does infinite possibility appear in my life?
3. What will improve and deepen my self awareness?
4. What is the truth of Tourmaline for me?

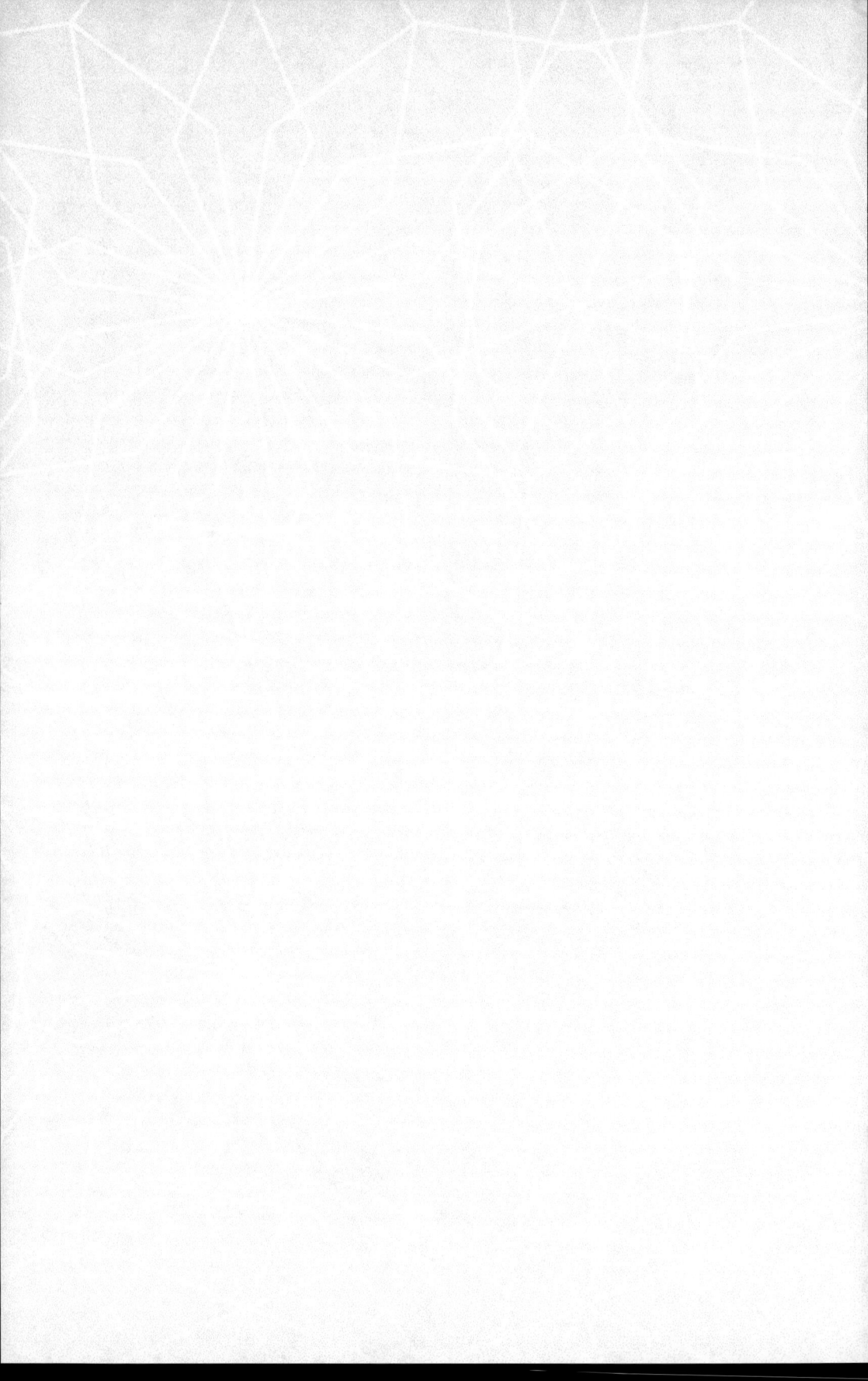

29

TURQUOISE
MOTHER

A precious stone of a sky-blue to apple-green color consisting of hydrous phosphate of aluminum with a cupric base. Originally found in the central Asian area referred to as Turkestan. The current spelling adopts the French form.

In the initial phase of my Akashic Records journey, I worked with Turquoise to move beyond my fear of speaking truth. My fear was focused toward the anticipated consequences – or more specifically, the feared results of saying out loud truth to another. Part of the fear came from my typical position within groups as the outlier, the weird one, the way-too perceptive one. For me, speaking truth had never been comfortable or safe. Now, faced with the enormity of the Akashic Records, I wanted to get right, to be safe in the telling, to not be ignored as crazy. All experiences which were normal for me especially when I broke my inner promise to never speak up or speak out. Within the Akashic Records, I wanted to experience freedom safely, and to be able to express fully as a witness. I began by wearing a necklace with a piece of turquoise sitting in the hollow of my throat. The intention was to allow support from turquoise to help me feel safe in expressing whatever came from the Records for me or through me. The shift was subtle. Over a month's time I noticed a firmness in. my voice and a new level of personal trust. Even to this day, I feel Turquoise's energy softly at my throat as I speak truth however it emerges.

Hello! I am so glad you are here. I am what you might think of as the Head Guardian, though I am more like Ancient Mother of Turquoise. Just refer to me as Mother Turquoise.

The energy of Turquoise is very precious and special. Before taking form, I went to a school of sorts and spent "time" learning about energy flows within Non-Physical Reality.

There is a motion in Non-Physical Reality which is focused entirely on resonance and balance. Within Non-Physical Reality this motion, the combined motion of resonance and balance, is one and the same. Physically this motion also appears as light and sound. Like many gemstones, Turquoise holds this motion both spiritually and physically.

The soul of Turquoise is expressed within the motion of resonance – especially the resonance of spiritual and physical. This is alignment at the foundation – at the beginning before there is physical expression.

My soul is one of foundation, of emergence into a new cycle, the experience which must happen for the Phoenix to rise. There is intentionally lightness both spiritually and in physical form to allow the initial movement to rise without interruption or hesitation.

My soul aligns with flow – the flow of water, of air, or fire and flame, of the breath of Akasha. My soul is of the movement of the photon as it begins to shine, to illuminate the path, to begin the soul's journey into deep expression. My soul is the arising of divine sound into the awareness of All That Is.

Turquoise is the energy flow of birth, of new beginnings, of light, of free, powerful expression.

There are many physical worlds in which I participate. Earth is one of these worlds. Each time I participate, I learn the agreements and I adjust my soul to accommodate and make best use of the agreements so that I may participate fully and with clear intention.

I have been part of each of Earth's incarnations and have worked with the Guardian Councils to fully express the resonance and harmony that is the foundation of my soul. This is part of what it means to be a gemstone.

My way of approaching resonance and harmony is to address obstacles to the flow, to the beginning and the initial arising.

I address hesitation and fundamental confusion. I assist the creative process with this intention and awareness. I hold space for easy, yet profound beginnings.

In any society where I have presence, I am there to support the beginning of motion in flow. I am there to be part of the circle of creation, the initiation of the cycle of conscious motion from spiritual to physical, from thought and feeling to physical manifestation of strength and unobstructed flow.

I also support the flow of clear speech and clear expression. For I am also about removing obstacles and removing interruptions.

I assist integration through a focus on resonance and harmony – though I see these both as reflections or aspects of integration.

Yet integration cannot be experienced when obstacle is encountered. Thus, I aid in the initial moments of movement when doubt can be crippling, when hesitation might become the entire expression.

There is possibility in each moment, and I support the realization, the opening to the possibility.

I am the motion of the first step, the motion of putting plan into action, for the initial flow of beginning.

I am the beginning and I support all beginning.

My message for humanity is simple:

Have no fear.
Begin in joy.

You know what you want. It is fear which stops you from making the effort to express, to engage, to experience.

Your focus on destination is mistaken as an idea of exactly where you must manoeuvre to obtain desire. This creates fear – fear of missing the mark, fear of failing to obtain or succeed, fear of pain along the way.

The fear becomes overwhelming, doubt and confusion arise, what was clear becomes clouded. You mistake this as failure, as proof of a self without value or worth.

I am affiliated with Ganesha, the remover of obstacles, with the colors blue and green. With the East as the beginning, the first step. Also with Ancient Mother, the emotion of Spring and the energy of spark.

I stand in the Temple of Light as one of the Guardians of the Journey and the arising of each soul. My energy is part of all beginnings.

Remember:

Have no fear.
Begin in joy.

Personal Exploration Questions from Turquoise:

Use these questions for journaling, contemplation, or meditation; open your Akashic Records or the Akashic Records of Turquoise and ask:

1. What can I do to release the obstacles in my life?
2. How do I ignore or deny the reality of my life?
3. How can Turquoise help me understand and speak truth?
4. What is the truth of my soul within the energy of Turquoise?

30

DIAMOND
PINNACLE OF RESILIENCY

A very hard and brilliant stone of crystalized pure carbon in regular octahedrons, either colorless or tinted. The hardest substance known.

I am the spokesman for Diamond!

I come to you from the beginnings. Diamond was part of the initial motion of Earth and, like Quartz, began without conscious awareness which is now maintained through the energy of a Gemstone Guardian.

Diamond is inherently about both reflection and refraction of light. Our light abilities and our solidity emerge through an intense process of stress and pressure. This personal experience of Diamond demonstrates the ability for any physical, energetic motion to resolve itself around the issue of pressure.

Pressure may be responded to in one of two ways. First: break. Second: fuse into more strength.

Breaking can feel awful, can feel like failure. Though, a break can be a process of reforming. In fact, breaks occur when the form under pressure has already begun the process of reforming along points of fissures. These are missing alignment and resiliency.

The presence of resilience is what allows pressure to yield increased strength.

To be resilient is to be able to allow the waves of life to raise you up rather than submerge you. This is not to say those with resiliency don't get swamped. Rather, those with resiliency are able to choose how and when to respond.

The resilient live within the constant awareness of choice. The resilient find a way to pick themselves up. The resilient forgo judgment on themselves and on others. The resilient know when the path forward requires breaking and reforming. The resilient aren't afraid of rising from the ashes, their inner essence reinvented.

As Diamond, my ability to sustain inordinate amounts of pressure to emerge into my final form gives me the energy to shine brightly, refract and reflect all light, and demonstrate, through the integration of body, mind, heart, and soul, how clarity is possible.

My clarity is filled with light and filled with an awareness of the light within all.

I realize I am known as the "Queen of Gemstones."

However, the hierarchy that this moniker implies is false pretense.

Because value and worth are inherent, comparing gemstones is false judgment. We each stand within the energy of incredible value.

My message to humanity:

Rise always into the best you can be and become.

If you can begin from this point of view, you can begin to seek to understand that which you don't understand. Instead of judging. Instead of pushing away what is unknown. Instead of unfairly criticizing and blaming others.

I am the demonstration of the unity of physical and spiritual integration.

The pressure which creates me is the same pressure you feel within yourself to understand who you are. This is the same pressure to embrace the power of who you are. The same pressure to feel capable and worthy to make your own choices.

Diamonds have an independent nature and will only be found when there is the desire to be found.

Because of our path of creation, we feel no compunction to be other than what we are.

We do not choose to live within a hierarchy. We instead choose to live within the connection existing within all creation.

For humanity to move forward, understand these basic ideas we hold as the essence of who we are as Diamond.

Remember:

Rise always into the best you can be and become.

Personal Exploration Questions from Diamond:

Use these questions for journaling, contemplation, or meditation; open your Akashic Records or the Akashic Records of Diamond and ask:

1. How can pressure help me build resiliency?
2. How am I like a diamond?
3. What steps can I take to experience the unity of my body, mind, heart, and soul?
4. What is the energy of Diamond for me?

READER BONUS

Working with the Gemstone Guardians, I have put together this free, downloadable PDF:

How to Work with Gemstone Energy
This is a printable PDF with five steps to connect and work with gemstone energy.

Also please know I have created a companion journal for you to use with the questions from all the Gemstone Guardians. This journal is available wherever books are sold. The paperback version has a black and white interior and the hard cover format has a full-color interior.

Plus, on my website, you may order a full color deck of healing cards based on the messages from Gemstone Guardians.

To find everything including the Reader Bonus PDF, check out this page on my website:

www.cherylmarlene.com/gemstone-guardians/

READY TO LEARN MORE?

Thank you so much for reading this book!

I am passionate about supporting you in your journey to find clarity and feel confident about who you are and who you can become.

For me, I write to share my truth in hopes you feel confident in finding and trusting your truth.

If you'd like to continue learning one-on-one, visit my website: **CherylMarlene.com**

Find a wide variety of spiritual consciousness and metaphysical articles, workshops, and workbooks at SpiritualDeepDive.com — when others skim, we dive!

If you would like to learn to access the Akashic Records with me, you have these options:

- **Books**: particularly *Akashic Records Masterclass*, shares how to open your Akashic Records and the Akashic Records of both human and non-human energy.

- *Akashic Record Insights*: weekly practices, workshops, workbooks plus a repository of information to expand your Akashic Records journey. Visit AkashicRecordsArchive.com

- **Akashic Records Intensive**: When you are ready, with me as your in-person guide, to go beyond stereotype into learning within the powerful depths of the sacred mysteries of the Akashic Records. Learn more and apply on my website.

These are all great options. Everything you need is there. Plus, you can add one-on-one student mentorship session when connecting directly with me calls to you.

Know that unlike a lot of places, all workshops, and especially the *Akashic Records Intensive*, are done in-person with me via Zoom. Videos are simply supplemental.

Whatever path your journey may take, may you experience and live within intrinsic truth, trust, and self-worth.

BELIEVE. Laugh. Learn. Love. Be. Become. Always.

In Joy!

Cheryl

ABOUT CHERYL

www.CherylMarlene.com

Cheryl Marlene is a pioneering guide in spiritual consciousness and the Akashic Records, blazing a new path for seekers ready to move beyond superficial answers. Her work is for those who desire unvarnished truth, deep transformation, and a profound connection to personal power.

A mystic, futurist, and trailblazer, Cheryl expands the Akashic Records beyond outdated myths into a living, dynamic spiritual practice, uniting divine and human consciousness in profound healing. Through one-on-one Akashic Record sessions, research, and future-driven business consulting, she helps clients and visionaries uncover their soul's wisdom and embrace their fullest potential.

As the creator of the *Akashic Records Intensive*, the most comprehensive Akashic Records training, and author of *Akashic Records Masterclass*, Cheryl challenges the limits of what's possible in spiritual innovation. Her students and clients know her as relatable, insightful, and unafraid of the raw and real aspects of deep work.

When she's not writing, Cheryl is on the hiking trail, listening to nature's wisdom and exploring the heartbeat of the mountain.

Through her journey, she has distilled her intention for life to these seven words:

BELIEVE. Laugh. Learn. Love. Be. Become. Always.

CherylMarlene.com

Bookstore.CherylMarlene.com

AkashicRecordInsights.com

SpiritualDeepDive.com

ALSO BY CHERYL MARLENE

Bookstore.CherylMarlene.com

———

Akashic Records Masterclass

Masterclass includes these four books which may also be purchased separately:

What are the Akashic Records?

Open Your Akashic Records

Open the Akashic Records for Other

500 Questions to Ask the Akashic Records

———

The New Akashic Records

Akashic Records: Gemstone Guardians

Gemstone Guardians Journal

How to Navigate the Five Steps of Your Spiritual Journey

Soul Compass: Trusting Inner Truth to Navigate Life's Uncertainties

Soul Compass Companion Journal

———

Spiritual Deep Dive Workshop-in-a-Book Series:

Understanding Doubt

Mastering Self Responsibility

Authenticity and the Soul

www.ingramcontent.com/pod-product-compliance
Lightning Source LLC
La Vergne TN
LVHW051229080426
835513LV00016B/1494